Julie Bindel is a journalist, author and feminist activist who has campaigned against male violence against women and girls since the age of seventeen. She has written extensively on rape, domestic violence, sexually motivated murder, prostitution and trafficking, child sexual exploitation, stalking and the rise of religious fundamentalism and its harm to women and girls. In 1990, Bindel co-founded Justice for Women, an organisation that supports, and advocates on behalf of, women who have been convicted of murder, when they have killed in circumstances of resisting male violence and abuse.

Bindel is the author of *Straight Expectations* (shortlisted for the Polari Prize) and *The Pimping of Prostitution*; she is also the co-author of *Exiting Prostitution* and *The Map of My Life: The Story of Emma Humphrey*, and has written numerous book chapters on violence against women, sexuality, gender and feminism.

T0004548

Praise for *Feminism for Women*

'Bindel speaks – in a voice that is resolute, undaunted after all these years . . . and if her text doesn't come with easy solutions to our problems, it is nevertheless guaranteed to remind us what we have still to fight for. I can't think of a single person who wouldn't benefit from reading it' *Observer*

'An impassioned manifesto' Kathleen Stock, *Spectator*

'Bindel makes a call to reset the feminist movement and resist the normalisation of sexual violence' *Guardian*

'Julie Bindel – one of the bravest, smartest journalists and campaigners out there – draws on a fearless lifetime on the front line of feminism and offers a refreshing, sometimes provocative, wake-up call for women of all ages' Samira Ahmed

'Bindel delivers a robust call to arms in every chapter . . . this book could not be timelier as the consequences of the coronavirus pandemic on women's lives become more stark . . . Feminism for Women should deliver hope to those who feel lost . . . Feminism for Women is a considered deconstruction of some of the myths pervading the modern feminist movement, and how, by going back to the basics, it can be fixed. As a young feminist who has finally seen the light, I consider it essential reading' *The Critic*

'Bindel's campaigning to end male violence is the rallying call men need to join the fight' David Challen

'Enlightening, infuriating and hopeful. Julie Bindel hits all the relevant points when it comes to feminism and what it means' Martina Navratilova

'Written for young feminists, it should be read by everyone. Bindel has rescued the story of radical feminism from airless conference halls and impenetrable Gender Studies courses specialising in erasing feminists and our histories' Gita Sahgal

'A sharply argued, deftly written examination of where feminism is at in 2021 – and where feminists should go next' Selina Todd

Feminism for Women

Women

The Real Route to Liberation

Julie Bindel

CONSTABLE

CONSTABLE

First published in Great Britain in 2021 by Constable
This paperback edition published in 2022 by Constable

3 5 7 9 10 8 6 4 2

A CIP catalogue record for this book
is available from the British Library.

ISBN: 978-1-47213-262-8

Typeset in Minion Pro by SX Composing DTP, Rayleigh, Essex SS6 7EF
Printed and bound in Great Britain by Clays Ltd, Elcograf, S.p.A.

Papers used by Constable are from well-managed forests
and other responsible sources.

Constable
An imprint of
Little, Brown Book Group
Carmelite House
50 Victoria Embankment
London EC4Y 0DZ

An Hachette UK Company
www.hachette.co.uk

www.littlebrown.co.uk

To the young feminists that dare

Contents

Preface

'Every time a woman stands up for herself, without knowing it possibly, without claiming it, she stands up for all women.'

Maya Angelou

'Feminism is not a fashion or a fetish: it's a liberation movement.'

Joan Scanlon

Right now, what passes for feminism is often anything but; it bends over backwards to accommodate the rights and feelings of men but leaves women out in the cold.

It would appear that feminism is the only social justice movement on the planet that is supposed to prioritise every other issue before pursuing its own objective: women's liberation. But this is a movement that centres women and girls and that is – and has to be – at the core of any meaningful definition of feminism. In this book I take it upon myself to define the term and I see the act of doing so as taking a political stand against the dilution of the term and all it stands for.

I therefore make no apology for defining feminism as I understand and practise it, and as I have used it all my adult life. The term may well be used by others to mean other things, and I expect to be challenged: after all, feminism, like any vibrant political movement, has always thrived on debate.

To me, feminism is a quest for the liberation of women from patriarchy. This is not only my personal definition: it comes from a history of collective activism, from a movement that includes women involved in grassroots campaigning, poorly educated women and women who have never been in the public eye.

This book is not addressing a sectarian crew of 'extremist' feminists, nor does it deal with 'niche' issues. It does not, I hope, speak to an echo chamber. These issues affect half of the planet. It is uncompromising because we are, I firmly believe, on the cusp of losing so many rights and freedoms we have won during the women's liberation movement.

Feminism is a quest for all women to be liberated from male supremacy, and an acknowledgement that women are a sex class oppressed by men as a sex class and not as individuals. Feminism resists and rejects the domination/subordination dynamic that inevitably emerges from hierarchy, in this case a sex hierarchy.

There is nothing natural or inevitable about our oppression as women, or men's power over us. Therefore, feminism is a utopian movement which imagines a possible world in which patriarchy is overturned and women are not oppressed. To this end, feminism supports and promotes women-only spaces, activism and consciousness-raising as methods to achieve the goal of women's liberation.

Feminism recognises that gender is distinct from sex. Gender is a social construct designed to impose rules of behaviour on women, also known as sex stereotypes. As the legal scholar and feminist Catharine Mackinnon says, 'The feminist theory of power is that sexuality is gendered and gender is sexualised. In other words, feminism is a theory of how the eroticised nature of dominance and submission creates gender, creates woman and man in the social form in which we know them. Thus the sex difference and the dominance-submission dynamic define each other.'

Feminism prioritises exposing and ending male violence towards women and girls. It also acknowledges that male violence is central to the ways and means in which men maintain control over and continue to oppress women. This includes all commercial sexual exploitation such as prostitution and the production of pornography, almost exclusively consumed by men.

Feminism recognises that *all* women are oppressed and forges a commitment to ending this oppression, while also recognising that oppression of women under patriarchy takes many different forms. None of us individually has experience of the varied forms of oppression endured by all women in every context, but collectively we do, and only together can we resist and overcome.

Feminism is, therefore, a collective movement, not an individual viewpoint. Fighting for women's 'rights' is not the same as fighting for women's liberation.

I believe that the definition I have outlined here will continue to enable women to progress radically in the direction of liberation. Over the decades, I have witnessed attempts to undermine, dilute and discredit this definition – by men and women. These attempts have always been motivated by the desire to prop up the status quo, not rock the boat, keep men happy, and keep women in their place. That is why I have relied on the above definition throughout my forty years in the movement and continue to do so.

In this book I will seek to deconstruct many myths about feminism by offering insights from decades of direct experience within the women's movement. I will report from a number of countries in both the Global North and the Global South, and from interviews with feminists, anti-feminists, young and older women, and even some men.

I would love for men to read this book and I do address them throughout, but perhaps not in the way that they are used to being addressed by feminists in recent years. Rather than making concessions in order that men feel more comfortable, I will be posing a direct challenge to those men to come up with ways in which they can support work we are doing to end male violence. Men can be feminist allies, and we could do with their help.

I hope to put forward suggestions for tangible solutions that will help women move forward to achieve our goal. One thing I will never compromise on is my belief that feminism has to refocus so that women are at the centre of the movement. We cannot remain an afterthought in our own political project, and yet that is what we are right now.

The issues I will explore throughout apply to women everywhere. As feminists, we are sick of the differences between women being rammed down our throats and used to divide us. It is not as if we are unaware of these differences, or the significance of them. Misogyny in the form of male violence, and the threat of male violence, affects us all. This book is about what unites us: the experience of being a sex class under patriarchy. It is also a call to arms on the basis of this common experience – and the desire to realise a world in which women are free from the reality and fear of male violence.

That is why this book is entitled *Feminism for Women*.

Introduction – The State We're In

'Many women, I think, resist feminism because it is an agony to be fully conscious of the brutal misogyny which permeates culture, society, and all personal relationships.'

Andrea Dworkin

My introduction to feminism came in 1979. I was a seventeen-year-old barely educated working-class lesbian who had moved from the north-east to the relatively big city of Leeds.

It was through feminism I quickly understood that my lesbianism was not a result of a faulty gene, nor was it anything bad or worrying. Through talking to the older feminists I met, I got to grips with 'compulsory heterosexuality', or the fact that female sexuality is controlled by men as a method to keep us in our place. I learned that lesbianism was seen as the ultimate transgression, which is what made it very dangerous and unacceptable; using the parlance of today, lesbians are the most 'gender non-conforming' people on the planet.

I came to see myself and other lesbians as sexual outlaws and warriors. Thanks to speaking with other feminists and recognising that I had internalised self-hatred because of the demonisation of lesbianism I slowly but surely stopped thinking of heterosexuality as 'natural' and thus stopped seeing lesbianism as unnatural or freakish.

Feminism was the very first political movement to critique heterosexuality and women's individual as well as collective relationship to men. As I came to further understand how the institution of marriage and the structure of the heterosexual family could be like a ball and chain for women, I also appreciated the benefits and pleasure of having escaped that future.

At the point I became active in the women's movement, in the late '70s and early '80s, there was a significant presence of lesbian feminists in the anti-violence-against-women campaigns of the time, including campaigns against the sex trade.

We realised, then as now, that the twin pillars of patriarchy and heterosexuality were inseparable, and you couldn't dismantle the former without challenging the latter. And that meant challenging the power and privilege of men, not just in the public sphere, but in their most intimate relationships and in their sexual attitudes towards women.

At that time the popularity of and easy access to pornographic films involved a rapid increase in the sexual exploitation of women and girls. Feminists began to make the connections between that exploitation – including the global sex trade – and the increased consumption by men of prostituted women filmed in pornography. We named it violence against women and rejected the liberal standpoint that women could be empowered by prostitution, and the myth that men and women are equal players in sex markets.

The vibrant and highly visible anti-porn movement in the UK throughout the 1980s included everyday campaigns against porn in the tabloid papers, which mobilised women who had never before been involved in any kind of feminist activism or protest.

This was the Thatcher decade, and an era of passionate protests against the new Conservatism, unemployment, individualism and renewed prejudice. It was also the period of the AIDS epidemic, and the ignorant and horrific stigmatisation of gay men. These political battles were fought on a number of different fronts – whether against nuclear weapons, pit closures, or new discriminatory legislation such as Clause 28 (which sought to prevent local authorities from providing any materials or education about 'alternative families'), to name but a few.

Lesbian feminists were visible in each and every one of these protests, whether at Greenham Common, in the Welsh mining communities, abseiling into the House of Commons, or chained to the leg of Sue Lawley's chair as she attempted to read the six o'clock news.

But our politics differed from those of gay men. They, for the most part, sought to be accepted by the establishment, assimilated into society and the institution of the family via marriage and adopting children. We wanted to confront and defy the establishment, and ultimately to bring about fundamental structural change and transform the lives of women.

The few feminist texts that emerged at that time were seized upon, devoured and debated hotly amongst us, and the ideas they generated were the oxygen of the women's movement. Andrea Dworkin's *Pornography*, Susan Brownmiller's *Against our Will*, Kate Millet's *Sexual Politics*, bell hooks' *Ain't I a Woman*, Kathleen Barry's *Female Sexual Slavery*, Germaine Greer's *The Female Eunuch*. Whether or not you agreed with

7

everything these writers said, their ideas were intimately inter-connected with the thinking that inspired feminist activism, and vice versa.

Central to our understanding of feminism was the relation-ship between gender and sexuality: we argued then, as now, that femininity was socially constructed to keep women subor-dinate to men, and that included everything from marriage to prostitution, from the beauty industry to the sex industry, from motherhood to monogamy. It was all up for discussion.

This was a time when there was a real connection between feminist theory and activism: even where there were heated arguments these only served to sharpen our thinking and our practice. It was also a time when women's lived experience was at the heart of the movement, and fundamental to our goal of liberation, not some abstract and contested theory of gender.

I had been aware of men's violence towards women and girls from a very young age having witnessed domestic violence within my extended family. Like so many other women, I had also experienced more than one incidence of sexual abuse and violence myself. The home is the most dangerous place for women and their children; it is where most male violence takes place. When I was growing up domestic violence was seen as a private affair, and rape in marriage didn't exist as a crime. The sexual abuse of girls by male relatives was simply pushed under the carpet, and also generally thought to be no one else's business, let alone a matter for intervention by the state.

Feminists were nonetheless raising awareness of these issues, not just domestic and sexual abuse, but also all forms of male violence, including that which was enacted through porn and prostitution. Because the threat and reality of male violence affects all women and girls, by focusing on this we convinced huge numbers of those normally hostile to feminists (or what they called 'women's libbers') to join us – or at least support our efforts.

Most men, however, didn't like us drawing attention to what they considered to be perfectly normal and reasonable behaviour: 'If you can't give your missus a slap when she's out of order, or tell a girl in the street she's got nice tits, what's the world coming to?'

The growing strength of women's voices on this subject – and the attack on what men saw as their rights – led to an inevitable backlash. And needless to say, 'man-hating' ugly lesbians were seen as the root cause of all the trouble.

Feminists are to blame for everything

Men with the ear of policymakers and government officials began to organise against the success of feminists in putting domestic and sexual violence on the agenda of the criminal justice system (CJS). Several men's rights organisations, such as Families need Fathers, were formed purely to protest against our demands that violent and sexually abusive men should not have access to their children. Hot on their heels came Fathers for Justice, and Mankind, followed closely by the False Memory Syndrome Society (FMSS). FMSS was, in many ways the most pernicious of the anti-feminist men's rights groups. Made up of wealthy, professional men, many of them psychiatrists, the FMSS existed to convince courts, policymakers and wider society that adults who disclosed sexual abuse as children were suffering from 'false memory syndrome' which had been put there by feminist therapists and counsellors hell-bent on falsely accusing men of heinous crimes.

These men, motivated by a desire to keep women in our place, made some progress in convincing senior figures within the CJS that feminists had exaggerated the scale and prevalence of male violence. Further, they were, to an extent, effective in persuading a number of naïve and ignorant officials that women were as likely to be the perpetrators of domestic violence and child abuse as were men. But with hard evidence and compelling survivor testimony, the feminists fought back, and we have continued to fight back against a sea of misinformation and false statistics, to persuade the CJS to prosecute perpetrators and protect victims, and to recognise the need for accurate information, knowledge and expertise in considering these cases.

Equality is not the goal

Alongside the vibrant decade of activism during the '80s, a sea change was taking place which led to the 'femocracy' of the '90s, as certain forms of feminist activism became institution-alised or corporatised.

The goal of women's liberation suddenly seemed to be replaced by the goal of equality, measured by how many women at the top had smashed the glass ceiling, and neglected those women for whom no door had ever been opened. At the same time, many grassroots women's organisations that had gained funding during the '80s became fearful of offending their stakeholders, and the form of feminism they espoused became tamer and less threatening to the establishment.

But there were still feminists who resisted this kind of assimi-lation, and feminist organisations who continued to fight for women's liberation. The 'sensible agenda', the feminist fight for childcare, equal pay, and all the self-evidently reasonable requests of the early women's movement faltered, but the radical agenda continued to forge ahead.

Justice for Women and other feminist organisations, such as Southall Black Sisters etc, which were set up to challenge male violence, remained resilient during these decades, and continued to be ever more inventive about ways of publicising their work and garnering support. By working with the media to publicise the cases of women who were killed as a response to male violence, and the numbers of rapes and sexual assaults against women, public awareness was continually being raised.

The new anti-feminism

By the beginning of the decade now described as the 'noughties', the effect of the internet on feminism was beginning to be felt in significant ways. I became preoccupied with the loss of face-to-face feminism, the lack of political meetings and protests, and the lack of any feminism driven by a sense of women's collective struggle.

I started to scour the internet for evidence that there was at least some kind of forum for feminist analysis and debate. What I found instead was what I call clicktivism, the presence of young women on message boards and zines, and the increasingly dominant presence of young men and trans women in these various forums. Moreover, we were told that this was to be welcomed, because, after all, feminism could only achieve its goals if they were in everyone's interests, primarily those of men, who would otherwise not give up their privileges willingly.

Frustrated with the lack of analysis and activism and dismayed by the rise of a new kind of identity politics informed by queer theory, I sought to publish a piece which challenged some of the new orthodoxies and reasserted the need for a theoretical framework based on the material reality of women's oppression as a sex class. In this article published in the *Telegraph* in 2003, I questioned the scientific basis for the latest diagnosis of transsexuality.

That is when I started to be targeted for particular attention, and it became clear how much anti-lesbian as well as anti-feminist and misogynist sentiment fuels that most vociferous section of the pro-trans lobby which has since had such a strong influence on the cultural debate about gender at large, and which has sought to undermine the theoretical under-pinning of feminism.

The internet, and the effects of globalisation, did produce some good outcomes for feminist activism in the early years of this century, not least by joining the dots of the global sex trade: feminists from the Global North were able to travel to India, the Philippines, the Balkans, and work with women from countries where those who were being trafficked into the UK were coming from. We started to make stronger connections and to work together more effectively, and we stopped using phrases like 'harmful cultural practices' and reaffirmed our common goal to challenge male supremacy and patriarchy in all its myriad forms.

But with the rise and rise of the queer movement outside of academic institutions, and the cementing of the new identity politics within (with men now becoming heads of feminist societies, and the bullying and no-platforming of any activist feminists) the last decade has seen feminism under attack once again. And it is no surprise that – once again – lesbian feminists are the main target of those who seek to undermine feminism.

This is a war which has been waged on many fronts, not least on the question of language. In the early days of the women's movement, feminists employed the term gender as a theoretical tool to describe the social construction of femininity and masculinity, the fabricated identities and sex stereotypes we wanted to dismantle and reject. We are now being told to forfeit that term, or to concede that it means the opposite – a biological phenomenon which determines our assumed identity. We are told that anyone who challenges this new orthodoxy is a TERF (trans exclusionary radical feminist) and a fascist. We are told we are on the wrong side of history, that the rights of trans women trump all other rights and we should be silent as natal women's rights are eroded.

The enemies of feminism have changed their tactics over time, and feminists have had to remain vigilant and become ever more inventive and resourceful to combat new obstacles in our fight for women's liberation. Sometimes anti-feminism is simply the old enemy in a new guise, and sometimes new enemies enter the battleground.

The Women's Liberation Movement, also known as Second Wave Feminism, emerged from the political left. There are countless examples from the UK and USA of women's resistance to male-left sexism. For example, at a leftist demonstration in Washington in 1969 to coincide with President Nixon's swearing-in ceremony, feminists demanded that they be given a voice to protest the sexism within the leftist movement. But when the women began to address the crowd, all hell broke loose from the men who shouted, laughed, heckled and booed. One bellowed: 'Take her off the stage and fuck her!' And another yelled: 'Fuck her down a dark alley!' The organisers, all men, simply led the women off the stage.

The hostility and bullying I faced as a young feminist came from deeply sexist men, women who found feminism threatening, and the far right.

The hostility and bullying that younger feminists have to deal with now comes primarily from the so-called progressives of their generation. They have all seen how prostitution (or rather 'sex-work' as it is rebranded), transgender ideology, and religious fundamentalism have been presented as part of a feminist philosophy, and have wondered: 'Why is this supposed to be feminist?' They have seen how porn is used as a form of sexual harassment and how it has been used to justify sexual assault. They wanted to be liberated from this culture of misogyny and believed feminism would help them achieve this, so they have gone back to the key feminist texts from an earlier era to find that clarity of analysis, and to inform their current politics. And they are reverting to methods of campaigning pioneered by first- and second-wave feminists, recognising the need to engage with real women and each other, to be physically present and to become more vocal, campaigning outside of online forums, many of which have become toxic spaces.

Alongside this, we have a global movement of sex-trade survivors and their allies, who are saying 'fuck off' to the sex-work narrative promulgated by those who benefit directly from the trade or profit indirectly as researchers, journalists, academics and publishers by promoting the libertarian view of prostitution. And yet here, to the astonishment of feminists in the Global South, we continue to have slut walks, and all those other queer-based protests, including women getting their tits out for men.

We have #feminism and #he4she initiatives which have made a big noise in the media and had lots of men cheering along but have achieved nothing concrete for women's liberation. And, thankfully, we still have active, materialist feminism, such as the creation of the Centre for Women's Justice, which is still fighting – with huge success – for the rights of women who have experienced male violence and been ill treated by the state.

As we enter a new decade, overshadowed by a health pandemic and another looming economic crisis, the effects of policies past and present are making themselves felt disproportionately in the lives of women, who always suffer most because they do the lion's share of the caring for children and the elderly, and because they are still clustered in the lowest-paid, most insecure jobs.

Challenging male violence

For those of us who still passionately believe that feminist activism is essential to achieve women's liberation, there is urgency about focusing once more on the material reality of women's lives. Repeated lockdowns have brought into sharp focus the escalating scale of domestic violence, and the deaths of women at the hands of male partners during Covid have increased exponentially. We cannot stand by and pretend that contemporary feminism is about how many women are on the board of the FTSE 100 companies, or about whether a girl of seven who wants to be a boy should be sent to the Tavistock.

All women, whether we are active feminists or not, need to understand exactly what is at stake for us if we lose our sex-based rights and remember that progress for women has never happened just through either the pressure of time, or men's enlightenment. It has happened through feminist activism.

We still have a long way to go before we achieve our aim of liberation, and therefore must continue to campaign for it even in this hostile environment and inhospitable climate, where women are routinely blamed for the sexual violence that we encounter, murdered by men that profess to love us, and advised to 'choke on a dick' if we dare share an opinion that sexist men object to on social media.

Some of this opposition comes from other women, which it always has, and we need to understand why that is but not be deterred by it.

Many women may not like feminism, or believe it is not relevant to them because they have built their lives primarily around having children and building a home and accepting an unfulfilling job. But what about maternity leave? Not every woman is eligible for it, but many are, and companies can be sued for not allowing women time off to have children, or not hiring a pregnant woman despite her suitability for the job. Those rights were won by feminists.

Many women don't feel comfortable around lesbians and think that feminism means having a go at heterosexual married women for making the choices they have. But heterosexual women are at least able to report their husbands to the police if they are violent, and could if necessary, escape to a women-only refuge. Whether or not they like or are involved in feminism, these rights affect them and their lives. So does the potential loss of these rights.

Violence against women is the main mechanism by which men control women the world over. Even a woman who has no experience of violence from her immediate partner is controlled by the fear of male violence from others and relies on the protection of men. Compulsory heterosexuality is not just about women being physically coerced into sexual relationships with men – such as forced marriage or corrective rape. It is about the mechanisms by which women themselves come to desire those relationships in order to be valued by men, deemed attractive by men, protected by men, and ultimately accepted by other women in society. Compulsory heterosexuality is a condition of patriarchy. Without patriarchy, heterosexuality would be a state women could freely choose. But you can be damn sure that in post-patriarchy there would be a significantly higher number of women who choose to be lesbians. Some of us are lucky enough to have figured that out some time ago – and I have never looked back.

Feminism is flourishing, as is the backlash to it. But whether or not you are a feminist, it is essential to understand that the misogyny so prevalent across the globe affects *all* women, whoever and wherever you are. In recounting an abridged version of my life as a feminist it is my intention not to individualise the issues I faced and campaigned around but to universalise them.

For instance, rape and sexual assault is a fact of life for women and girls everywhere. The NGO Equality Now found ten countries that currently allow spousal rape: Ghana, India, Indonesia, Jordan, Lesotho, Nigeria, Oman, Singapore, Sri Lanka and Tanzania. In four of these countries sex with a child is permitted, at any age, if she is married to the perpetrator.

But, if you are reading this whilst living in the UK and are tempted to feel reassured at the situation because rape in marriage was made a crime, thanks to feminists, in 1991, think again.

Of the tiny minority of rapes that are actually reported to police only 1.4 per cent are charged by the Crown Prosecution Service (CPS). How many of those convictions are of men married to their victims?

A survey commissioned by the End Violence against Women Coalition in December 2018 found that more than a third of over-sixty-fives do not consider forced marital sex rape, along with 16 per cent of people aged sixteen to twenty-four. That's a quarter of Britons who believe that non-consensual sex within marriage does not constitute rape.

A woman reporting rape five years ago had a much better chance of seeing justice done. How can it be that we have moved so far backwards in a crime that is so serious and does so much harm? Of course the situation in countries that permit child marriage, or flog a rape victim to death because she is seen to have 'dishonoured' her family, is worse than in those where such practices are not normalised or legalised. But how is it that child sexual abuse in the UK *is* often normalised? When the BBC presenter and serial sex offender Jimmy Savile had sex with thirteen-year-old girls they were subsequently described not as victims of rape, but 'groupies'. And look at the Rotherham grooming scandal. An independent inquiry found that a minimum of 1,400 children had been sexually abused by adult men, and pimped out all over the country, but a number of police officers and social workers simply wrote the abuse off as the girls having made 'poor lifestyle choices'.

The odds are really stacked against women quite significantly. The appalling lack of convictions for rape could not happen in a climate where women were respected. Women are seen as worthless and judged for 'getting themselves raped' because the men that actually commit these crimes are hardly ever held accountable for their actions. Indeed, more effort appears to be put into excusing rape than condemning the rapists.

It's too easy for people to dismiss those of us who centre the battle to end male violence as strident man-haters and irrelevant second-wavers, especially when so many young women are told that second-wave feminism was just a load of privileged white women being essentialist and bigoted, and that it made no difference to the majority of women outside of the movement. The current hostility is more brutal than any I have encountered over the past forty years.

Men have always told women to 'chill out' about issues such as pornography and sexual violence, but what is new – and particularly shocking – is that now many women who label themselves feminist are saying the same.

Under this rebranded feminism it is acceptable, if not obligatory, for young, 'progressive' men to refer to older feminists as 'Nazis', and 'fascists' even though the women they are insulting are the ones who have spent their whole lives fighting to end male violence and to support women. We are told we are irrelevant, cancelled and the opposite of what passes as feminist in today's confused world.

Reasserting feminism

A dialogue about what feminism means has always been part of the women's movement. With the number of misleading and inaccurate definitions creeping into popular use, it is more vital than ever that we define feminism as a political movement, a political movement to change the distribution of power.

Without a clear definition, we don't have the basis for our campaigning and demands. If feminism is how any individual defines it, then we have already lost the battle. Can you imagine socialists saying, 'Socialism is whatever one who opposes capitalism feels like identifying as socialism'?

Black Lives Matter makes the excellent point that it is not enough for white people to be 'non-racist' but that they should commit to being 'anti-racist'. The same could be said for feminism – it's not enough to be non-sexist, you have to commit to being anti-sexist.

In this book I want to argue for a clear definition of feminism as liberation for women, and invite anyone who thinks that is misguided to challenge me. Feminism is not a lifestyle choice but a movement with specific goals. It is not about who has the authority to define feminism, but about understanding the urgency with which we need that definition.

The reinvention of the terms 'sex' and 'gender' means that people are at best confused and at worst led to believe that all sexual minorities and a multiplicity of genders should be subsumed under the banner of feminism, and that it's a human rights violation to challenge this. 'Gender' – which feminists have always sought to abolish because it is the imposition of sex stereotypes on girls and women – is now dressed up and handed back to us as an immutable individual identity. At the same time, women are under pressure to deny the biological reality of our bodies and to use terms such as 'chest feeding' for breastfeeding and 'front hole' for vagina. Even the term 'woman' is in danger of becoming obliterated in favour of 'menstruater', 'womb-haver', and 'non-man'.

How can we identify sexism if we can't even agree what sex is? What does 'women's liberation' mean if we can't agree what a woman is?

If the term 'woman' is up for grabs and means 'any human who identifies as such', then what's the point of fighting for our liberation? If men can simply say that they are women based on a mere 'feeling', then what exactly *does* it feel like to be a woman? I'm a woman but I have no idea. I only know what it feels like to be *treated* as a woman under patriarchy.

Young women in universities and other settings are being silenced and bullied into accepting a form of feminism that benefits men and is harmful to women. Of the many women under the age of thirty who I interviewed for this book, every single one of them had a similar story of being told that they are racist/transphobic/bigoted/anti-sex/whorephobic and homophobic for simply stating the basics of feminism. These basics include the facts that women have the right to organise autonomously; that prostitution is dangerous; and that gender is a harmful social construct that promotes sex stereotypes and maintains women's subordination to men.

Feminists have never denied the biological differences between men and women but have always resisted those differences being used as a reason to abuse and demean us.

Feminists don't care if men want to dress and identify as women: what we care about is protecting our sex-based rights and services, particularly in women's refuges and prisons.

The political consequences for women in losing our single-sex spaces are severe, and recognising biological sex (as distinct from gender identity) is important when we look at crime statistics, especially sex crime. In 2019, Freedom of Information requests uncovered the fact that, in more than ten police forces across the UK, if a man is arrested for or convicted of rape, the official record will state 'the gender they chose to identify themselves as' before putting 'male' or 'female', regardless of whether or not that person has intact male genitalia.

The campaign by Stonewall UK and other trans rights organisations to amend the Equality Act 1975 to remove the right to single-sex services has failed. This reversal has come about because of feminist campaigning, not bigotry, and is a perfect example of how feminists can never rest on our laurels: women are *always* in danger of losing our rights. As Taina Bien-Aimé, executive director of the Coalition against Trafficking in Women (CATW) says, in a world where it is seen as perfectly acceptable and legal to buy and sell women's bodies, 'we can't possibly know what it means to have indivisible rights, universal rights and inalienable rights'.

The 57 varieties of feminism

In the past three years especially, feminism has been spinning off into a dizzying number of subsidiaries: Power feminism. Victim feminism. Equality feminism. Difference feminism. Post-feminism. Third Wave feminism. Post-patriarchal feminism.

Our anti-porn stance has led to us being accused of being aligned with Christian fundamentalists and the right wing, something that has only increased more recently in relation to trans activism. And yet our analysis of wanting structural change and fighting for the rights of oppressed groups makes us much more politically aligned with the left (although the reality of actual campaigning is that men on the left will not support an agenda that is about liberating women because it is not in their interests.)

These days, practically every politically engaged left-leaning woman, along with a significant number of men, describes herself as feminist, to the point that the feminist community and the progressive community have become essentially the same thing. There is no longer any expectation that being a feminist requires you to do anything feminist whatsoever; feminism has been rebranded and repackaged as a 'just be kind and nice to everyone' cause.

But promoting the sex trade and men's use of pornography and prostituted women is not feminist. Defending sadism and masochism just because somebody has an orgasm is not feminist. Claiming that a lesbian is transphobic for rejecting a penis, 'despite' it being attached to a trans woman, is definitely *not* feminist.

The gender madness has even seeped into the animal rights movement. Feminist writer Mary Kate Fain joined an animal rights group in Washington DC and was reprimanded by a non-binary member who told her it was 'hurtful' to hear Fain describe the abuse of female cows in the dairy trade. The non-binary member said: 'You're not allowed to say dairy comes from female cows or eggs come from female chickens because we don't know their gender identity.'

Feminism is for *all women*, but not all women are feminist. That does not mean, however, that they should not benefit from women's liberation in the same way as the women fighting to end male supremacy will. As the activist and writer Andrea Dworkin wrote: 'Feminism is a political practice of fighting male supremacy on behalf of women as a class, including all the women you don't like, including all the women you don't want to be around ... they all have the same vulnerability to rape, to battery, as children to incest.'

We're not done yet

The irrefutable figures from governments to rape crisis and domestic violence helplines and shelters about the extent of male violence and abuse seem to cut no sway with those who insist that feminists moan in order to put the fear of god in other women, which in turn hinders them from living fulfilled lives. But then, throughout history, feminists have always been told to 'shut up and go home'.

After the vote was won on equal terms in 1928, suffragists and suffragettes were informed that there was nothing left to do and any further feminist activism was sneered at – despite the fact that the suffrage campaign was never just about the vote and included the fight for equal pay, access into certain professions closed to women, the right to be legal guardians of their own children and exposing the extent of male violence.

After World War Two, having briefly been recruited into work and public life to support the war efforts while the men were away, women were told to get back in the house and remember their real place: the home.

Just as the suffrage movement (which was itself a loose coalition of uneasy bedfellows) did not achieve women's equality, so the achievements of the Women's Liberation Movement do not yet constitute the achievement of women's liberation.

The gains that we have made are not the end of the road. They are merely small steps along the way to the ultimate goal and although feminism has achieved huge amounts, we still can't see the finishing post.

Male violence towards women and girls is still a global reality. Conviction rates for rape are at an all-time low. Trafficking of women across borders for the purposes of prostitution is a thriving trade. The porn industry finds newer and more insidious methods in which to make money from the abuse of women for male sexual gratification.

With the younger generation of women facing forms of sexual coercion via technological advances in the promotion of pornography that we could not have imagined in our worst nightmares, the need for feminism has never been more urgent.

Done properly, feminism can be a dangerous business and women are often punished severely for speaking out. In June 2020, the world-famous novelist and philanthropist JK Rowling was denounced by extreme trans activists and their allies for simply objecting to the term 'menstruator' and for stating that biological sex is a reality.

In December 2018, the tennis legend and lesbian Martina Navratilova took a stand against the inclusion of male-bodied trans athletes competing against women in sports. 'There must be some standards and having a penis and competing as a woman would not fit that standard,' Navratilova tweeted. 'What are you afraid of, getting a backlash on Twitter? Those of us that can speak out need to do so. There are plenty of women who can't.'

Neither Rowling nor Navratilova appear to have any intention of being cowed by the bullies for exposing misogyny and defending the meaning of the term 'woman'. Both have wealth and power and they have chosen to align themselves with women everywhere to fight for the rights that are so precarious.

In the 1980s, feminism was rebranded as toxic, man-hating and totally mad. Today it is in vogue. Everyone claims the label and yet much of what passes for feminism continues to be nothing but pandering to men and their needs.

Yet the authentic meaning and goal of feminism is the liberation of women from male supremacy. Patriarchy is real and tangible – and no woman, whatever her privilege or lack of, can avoid or easily deny it.

Chapter 1

Are We Nearly There Yet? Has Feminism Achieved Its Goals?

'... it seems to me fairly obvious that the world is unfair to women because they are women. Why isn't everybody angry?'

Chimamanda Ngozi Adichie

Lest We Forget

On 8 December 1989 a disparate group of feminists gathered in Trafalgar Square, Central London, holding placards and banners aloft, chanting through loudhailers and stamping our feet to stay warm.

The demonstration was in response to the murder of fourteen female engineering students in Montréal two days earlier, which was almost immediately dubbed the Montréal Massacre. The killer, Marc Lépine, specifically targeted women at the engineering school within the École Polytechnique, claiming feminists had ruined his life.

This was before the internet, email or mobile phones. But feminists knew how to organise, and we had networks around the country. We shared friendship and political networks, as well as running domestic violence refuges and rape crisis centres. The Women's Liberation newsletters were produced by hand in the home of whoever had the biggest kitchen table on which to lay out the pages.

In order to confirm the details of what had happened at the École Polytechnique, I telephoned a woman in Montréal who explained that the entire Canadian media had decided that the killer was mentally deranged. 'Feminists understand that the motive was simply misogyny,' she said.

The protest was arranged by word of mouth. The banners, adorned with the names of the fourteen victims, were made on the floor of my kitchen. We had no office, no funding and no staff. The placards were recycled from those for a recent Lesbian Strength march that had been stored in my wardrobe, and we painted over 'Lesbians are everywhere!' with 'Male violence is terrorism', 'End Male Violence' and 'Misogyny Not Madness'.

We knew that it was about hatred of women and a backlash to the achievements of feminism in Canada, such as a recent victory on abortion rights. As a response to such victories, the men's rights movement was gathering pace.

At first the Canadian press, police and public intellectuals insisted that this was a story of a madman – a lone wolf, a crazed individual. Female journalists I met in Montréal told me that they were sent out by their male editors to find out what had 'made him this way' and 'what happened in his child-hood'. It was the same by the time the story hit the UK press, three days after the massacre. *The Times* headline read, 'Montréal killer was incited by "rejections"' and the *Independent* ran 'Montréal killer had unhappy love life'.

In 2012 I was invited to Montréal by a feminist organisation to speak at the memorial event on 6 December on male violence and women's resistance. The event was packed with feminists, human rights activists, and a number of grieving relatives of the murdered women. 'Never again,' we chanted, wishing it were true.

During my trip I met the journalist and feminist Francine Pelletier in Montréal, who told me that a year after the massacre she was sent a copy of Lépine's suicide note which had been found in his clothing. He explained his political motivations and listed eighteen women he wanted to kill, including feminist figures, the first female police officer, the first woman fire-fighter, and a number of anti-sexist men. Pelletier was also on that list.

The year after my first visit to Montréal, renowned scholar, lifelong feminist campaigner and close personal friend Janice Raymond (who had long been targeted as 'transphobic' on the strength of a book entitled *The Transsexual Empire* published in 1979) was invited to speak at the 2013 memorial about her work to combat sexual exploitation of women and girls around the globe. Trans activists did their best to get the event cancelled and, when they failed, organised a large protest during the speeches in memory of the murdered women.

Lépine was the first public Incel (Involuntary Celibates – men who blame women for their own failings). His hatred of women and warped sense of entitlement was born of the misogynistic, patriarchal culture in which he was raised. Today, the Incel movement is populated by many thousands of men who meet online and plot revenge against women.

Nathalie Provost was shot by Lépine during the massacre but survived. I met her during a subsequent trip to Montréal and she told me she recalls the murderer shouting that the women were studying engineering because they were 'all feminists'. She answered him back, saying they were not, in the desperate hope he would let her go. He shot her anyway. As Andrea Dworkin said at a memorial event for the fourteen murdered women: 'It is incumbent upon each of us to be the woman that Marc Lépine wanted to kill. We must live with this honour, this courage. We must drive out fear. We must hold on. We must create. We must resist.'

Every day, in every country in the world, women die at the hands of men. But sometimes, women fight back against male violence.

As I squeezed on to the press bench at the Royal Court of Justice in London, I glanced up at the packed public gallery. Dozens of feminist campaigners eagerly awaited the decision of three Appeal Court judges in the landmark case of Sally Challen. I looked over at her lawyer, my partner Harriet Wistrich, and caught her eye. We were both thinking about another Justice for Women murder appeal that had been held in that same court almost a quarter of a century before.

Emma Humphreys' childhood had been dominated by violence and abuse. She was sixteen years old when she killed Trevor Armitage in 1985. He was her violent boyfriend and pimp, and on this occasion she had armed herself against yet another rape. She was convicted of his murder in 1986. The original jury was not allowed to consider the history of sexual violence or the context of Humphreys' life. But seven years later, with the backing of Justice for Women (JfW), the campaign for her release began.

Three years after she first contacted JfW, Humphreys won her appeal and walked out of court to hundreds of cheering supporters. Her victory made headlines all over the world and her case resulted in a change in the law. Judges could now direct juries to take into consideration the whole life histories of women who ended up on trial for murder in such cases. But listening to Sally Challen's appeal in February 2019, I wondered why, in the many years since we had won the campaign to free Emma Humphreys, women such as Sally were still having to fight the same battle.

I looked towards her family in the public gallery and saw her younger son David, who had campaigned not only for his mother's release but also against domestic violence in general. I struggled to remain impassive as we awaited the judges' decision because my heart was in my mouth. When I heard the presiding judge say, 'This appeal is granted,' it was hard not to jump up and start cheering.

Sally had been convicted of murdering her husband Richard in August 2010. She had battered him to death with a hammer and then driven to the notorious suicide spot Beachy Head. She was talked out of jumping but immediately arrested.

While in prison, trying to cope with how she had finally responded to her husband's four decades of cruelty and abuse, Sally gradually realised that she had also been psychologically tortured throughout her marriage.

The absence of a bloody nose or black eyes meant that, under current legislation and in terms of public awareness at that time, she was not seen as a victim of domestic violence. It was quite some time after her arrest that she disclosed that Richard had anally raped her as punishment for one of his friends forcing a kiss on her; this brutal act of sexual violence and humiliation was merely one incident in a catalogue of sustained abuse, from physical to mental punishment, from extreme violence to psychological attrition.

One Christmas he sent cards to friends and family members showing him sitting on the bonnet of his Ferrari with his legs spread wide, topless women on either side of him. Sally had also discovered that Richard was going to a brothel close to her place of work, and she learned from TV news reports that the police had raided the establishment and found trafficked women there. She was understandably appalled.

The couple separated briefly, but in early 2010, Richard forced Sally to sign a humiliating agreement in which he only agreed to reconcile if she promised not to interrupt him or answer him back, and never to speak to strangers during a night out. Consequently, at her initial trial, she was painted as a jealous, spiteful wife taking revenge on her husband for having affairs.

Sentenced to a minimum of twenty-two years in prison, Sally's mental health deteriorated further, and locked up, away from her beloved sons and support network, she tormented herself with the reality of what she had done.

Having spent a year in prison, in 2011 Sally was offered a lifeline. JfW received a letter from her cousin, who explained that Sally had been poorly represented at her initial trial and also catalogued the decades of abuse she had endured at Richard's hands. Despite the complexity of finding new legal grounds to challenge the conviction, JfW rose to the challenge. We began campaigning to raise awareness about the case and found lawyers who not only understood sexual and domestic abuse but were willing to take it on pro bono while they found grounds on which to lodge an appeal.

Four years after Sally was convicted of murder, a new law of 'coercive control' was added to the statute, making it a criminal offence for the first time. Feminists had long campaigned for this new law, having recognised that some men choose largely non-violent methods to hold their victims captive and make them totally compliant to their demands.

She is now a free woman and, along with her son David, JfW and other feminist organisations, continues to campaign to end male violence.

One step forward ...

Over the past five decades of feminism, many of our most successful campaigns have focused on male violence towards women and girls. It was a bedrock of the second wave and now male violence against women and girls is firmly on the legal agenda. Social attitudes regarding sexual and domestic violence have undergone a revolutionary change.

Why, then, do so many women still end up dead at the hands of violent men? How is it that conviction rates are so low that rape has more or less been decriminalised? Despite feminism's achievements, in many significant ways our rights as women have been rolled back to the dark ages.

In 1980, the year I first met feminists who were campaigning to end sexual assault, one in three reported rapes ended in a conviction. In 2020, the conviction rate is one in every sixty-five.

Quite simply, men are getting away with rape – unless, of course, you think that the vast majority of women who report rape to the police are lying; certainly, some police and prosecutors still believe that huge swathes of women make false allegations. In recent years, there has been a worrying increase in the number of women being arrested and then cautioned or charged with making false allegations of rape. For example, in 2014, it was found that 109 women had been prosecuted for false rape claims in five years.

In the meantime, while the CPS appears to enthusiastically charge women with making false allegations, rape has been more or less decriminalised in recent years. The proportion of rapes reported to the police that result in a charge by the CPS has fallen to a record low of 1.4 per cent. Around 60 per cent of those result in a conviction, which means a conviction rate of under 1 per cent of those reported – known to be the tip of the iceberg when it comes to the numbers of rapes *actually committed*. Indeed, the CPS's own figures from July 2020 show that complainants face only a one in seventy chance of their case being charged.

The first time I campaigned directly on this issue was in 2006, after an eighteen-year-old woman contacted me with a terrible story. Ayesha, a British Asian woman living in London, had gone into a secluded area of her local park to have sex with her boyfriend. Unbeknown to her, once they were in the park the boyfriend then texted two of his friends and invited them to join in.

The men filmed themselves raping Ayesha. After she escaped, badly injured and shaken, she reported the crime to the police. The men were arrested and interviewed under caution but, when the police saw the video footage, they decided it showed a young woman having consensual sex with three men.

The police accused Ayesha of wasting their time and issued her with a caution, warning her that if she did not accept it, she could be charged and taken to court for perverting the course of justice. Having been referred to a feminist lawyer, and with the support of Justice for Women, Ayesha challenged the caution and had it retracted.

Thirteen years later, in 2019, an eighteen-year-old British woman called Emily* went on a working holiday to Ayia Napa in Cyprus, prior to starting university. One night, Emily was having sex with her holiday boyfriend Sam in his hotel room when a gang of up to twelve of his friends entered the room and began filming them. Emily can be heard on the film telling them to 'get out'. Several of the gang then had sex with her. Emily, who sustained well over two hundred injuries that night, went to the police and reported having been gang raped. The youths were arrested but, after seeing the video footage, the police concluded that Emily had had consensual sex with all the men.

Having been asked to return to the police station to 'clarify' a few things in her statement, Emily was hounded into signing a retraction and denied the opportunity to make a phone call or have a lawyer present. She was then arrested for the crime of public nuisance (the Cypriot equivalent of wasting police time) and sent to prison for more than four weeks before being released on bail. Finally, after months of waiting in Cyprus and having had her passport confiscated, Emily was found guilty and given a suspended sentence.

I visited Emily and her mother in Cyprus in December 2019, just before her trial, and interviewed them both. I have absolutely no doubt that Emily was telling the truth. She endured a gang rape and reported the crime to the police, and yet she was the one who ended up being imprisoned and treated as a criminal.

Figures show that in the period between March 2018 and March 2019 convictions for rape were at the lowest since the 1970s. Only one in sixty-five reported rapes resulted in a conviction. However, in the past decade at least two hundred women in the UK have been prosecuted for lying about being raped. Most of these women were sent to prison, with many receiving sentences of two or more years. Prosecutors went after teenagers, women with mental health issues, women who had experienced past physical and sexual assault, and women who were grappling with drug and alcohol addiction.

Kate Ellis is a solicitor at the Centre for Women's Justice (CWJ), a legal charity set up in 2016 with an aim of calling the state to account for failures in dealing with male violence. I asked for her views on why the police, along with the entire criminal justice system, seem unable to deal adequately with sexual assault allegations. She feels there is an 'alarming regression' in the way that the UK criminal justice system responds to violence against women *per se*.

The charity is constantly being referred cases in which women and young girls are absolutely distraught because they have gone to the police with a legitimate expectation that the ordeal that they have been through will have consequences for the attacker. But more often than not, it is the victim who suffers the consequences of reporting her assault to the legal system while the attacker carries on his life with no harm done to him. The victim is either let down by the system because she is disbelieved or has her case discontinued or feels humiliated when her mobile phone and social media accounts are scrutinised during evidence gathering.

I am also regularly contacted by women who have reported their sexual assault to the police but had their experiences minimised and disbelieved. Unsurprisingly, this makes it much harder for those women to recover from the original trauma. 'The authorities can't charge every single case,' says Ellis, 'but when less than two per cent of all complaints made are being prosecuted, something has gone badly wrong.'

Lisa Avalos, a law professor based in the USA and an expert in sexual assault investigations, has written extensively about women charged with and convicted of making false allegations of rape in the UK and USA. She tells me: 'Many victims, upon learning that police are sceptical of them, will retract a complaint in order to end contact with police and get themselves to a place of physical and emotional safety. As one victim of this practice said to me, "He [the policeman] made me feel like the only way out was to say it didn't happen. I just wanted to get out of that room and away from the detective."'

I can understand this. I doubt I, a seasoned feminist campaigner, would report rape or sexual assault to the police in the current climate of police and CPS scepticism and relative inaction.

It is a topic that has been raised time and again, but the casual manner in which male attackers so frequently walk free from accusations of sexual violence or assault is so often linked to the wider glorification of female abuse. And this has been seen for decades in porn.

Pimping pornography

The way in which the pornography industry has expanded and evolved is another example of how much more there is to do before feminists can pack up and go home.

Throughout the 1980s and 1990s, a vibrant anti-porn feminist movement swept across the UK. There were conferences on the harms to women and girls, and direct actions against sex shops took place on a regular basis, such as supergluing the locks shut and graffitiing the windows in the middle of the night.

In the past two decades, however, 'progressives' have rewritten the narrative and been given carte blanche to smear those who campaign against it as sexless harridans. Suddenly stripping becomes 'empowering', prostitution is sanitised as 'sex work', pornography becomes 'sexual freedom', and being choked and spat at during sex is declared to be a 'kink', which in turn is 'sex positive'.

Alongside this the porn industry has been transformed and is no longer just about magazines and sex shops and cinemas – it's worth billions of dollars and is a key driver of technology. The pornography I campaigned against as a young feminist is now being broadcast throughout the day on music TV channels, and pre-teenagers can easily view what we used to call hardcore porn on their smartphones.

The writer Linda Grant told me that when she began writing *Sexing the Millennium: A Political History of the Sexual Revolution* (1993) nearly thirty years ago, a key debate in feminism was about whether or not pornography was harmful to women. There was much discussion as to whether or not it could be controlled and limited.

'It seemed possible that there were ways to ringfence porn, a concept which seems now to be a sandcastle washed away by the mighty sea,' says Grant. 'Porn has pervaded every aspect of our lives, accessible to everybody including small children. I can't imagine being a girl growing up with sadomasochistic porn being watched by a group of eight-year-old friends, but that's the reality and nobody knows the consequences.'

In the mid-1980s, I travelled to a number of cities around England to speak at meetings of feminists who were keen to campaign against pornography and who wanted to look at what they were protesting against in a safe environment. I brought a slideshow of images, which started with the topless models that usually graced the centrefold of *Playboy* and ended with a copy of the infamous *Hustler* cover that depicted a lifelike image of a naked woman being pushed through a meat grinder. A handful of women always left the room upset.

Speaking with a group of fourteen-year-old girls during an International Women's Day event at their school in March 2020, I was told that these days violent pornography is an everyday reality for most girls. Gemma* told me, 'I get dick pics all the time, and one boy sent a video around the school of him having sex with a girl that he said was me, but it wasn't. He did that because I said I wouldn't have sex with him. I know that this kind of thing happens to most of my friends as well.'

Gail Dines, feminist campaigner and author of *Pornland* (2010), is also the director of Culture Reframed, an NGO that provides advice and support for parents who want to talk about porn with their teenagers. She tells me that she is not surprised that girls are being subjected to sexual harassment via online porn: 'Boys have been taught that porn can be used as a weapon against girls, and that they can access it with the tap of a smartphone.'

Although proving a causal connection is difficult, there is plenty of evidence-based research that suggests that the more porn boys and men consume, the more likely they are to be sexually aggressive to women and girls. The internet has made hardcore porn more affordable, accessible and anonymous: the main drivers that increase demand. Using porn today is a rite of passage and women are the collateral damage of this shift.

The late Andrea Dworkin, author of *Pornography: Men Possessing Women* (1979), anticipated in that book how much more extreme and readily available pornography would become if left unabated. As she said to me shortly before her death in January 2004:

'Once pimps and pornographers get a sense of how much money is to be made out of selling women's pain they will always find new ways to expand the market.'

But Dworkin could never have imagined where technology would lead the industry. Increasing numbers of men are documenting their sexual activities on social media, often including their assaults on women and girls. Raised on a diet of hardcore porn, when these men assault women they are re-enacting the porn they have watched on sites such as Pornhub, as well as generating content for the platform.

The increased use of porn, and the level of violence and abuse portrayed within it, is surely a reflection of the level of misogyny that women and girls are experiencing in everyday life. Why else would so many boys and men of all ages and demographics want to masturbate to images of women being humiliated, tortured and abused? How can this not be an indication of the way that men are encouraging each other to view women?

Whose revolution?

The mainstream narrative is that the sexual revolution significantly changed things for the better for women. But often the appearance of revolution is not real revolution.

For Sheila Jeffreys, an academic and the author of *Anticlimax: A Feminist Perspective on the Sexual Revolution* (1990), it was solely about men's sexual liberation. 'It paved the way for the construction of the industries of pornography and prostitution that serviced men's sexual desires to use reluctant women forcefully and often furiously over recent decades,' she says. 'The porn that it unleashed promoted many abusive forms of male sexual behaviour towards women and made them seem normal, such as sadomasochism, strangulation and anal sex.'

Rosie Boycott, who edited Britain's most famous feminist magazine *Spare Rib* in the 1970s, is similarly scathing: 'What was insidious about [the revolution] was that it pretended to be alternative. But it wasn't providing an alternative for women. It was providing an alternative for men in that there were no problems about screwing around.'

Of course, the availability of the contraceptive pill was hugely beneficial to women, as for the first time they could have hetero-sexual sex free of risk, but there were negative consequences too. As the journalist and feminist Beatrix Campbell says, 'Before the pill, girls and women would be told, "Don't be left with a burden [baby]", and mothers everywhere were on a mis-sion to protect their daughters from unwanted pregnancy. But what it [now] promised men was risk-free sex with all women, any women, any time. The sexual revolution, rather than being great for us, merely maximised men's access to women.'

Campbell believes that the pill put an end to the sexual pleasure derived from foreplay because there was no longer any viable excuse not to allow penetrative sex. She says: 'Men knew they could do what they wanted with women who no longer had the excuse of "I might get pregnant".' The sexual revolution did not result in the removal of stigma for women who showed any indication of enjoying sex. It was, and still is, assumed that such women are 'slags' and fair game.

The rules have always been different for men; for them, having lots of sex with multiple women is considered 'healthy' and, with the current low conviction rate for reported rapes, they know it is not just likely but probable that if they commit rape, they will get away with it. The myth that hordes of women 'cry rape' is difficult to sustain when those who report sexual assault are rarely taken seriously, particularly sexually active young women who drink alcohol.

But how is it that so many young women today are mistaking their own exploitation for freedom?

Defending dangerous sex

A number of young feminists tell me that challenging the pornified culture that promotes the eroticisation of sexual violence can lead to hostility. 'I frequently had to explain and justify my beliefs before entering into discussion about things like prostitution and pornography; gender being oppressive and a construct; and how women's oppression is a material reality,' says student Anna-Louise about her unhappy time in her university's feminist society.

Louise Perry is a feminist writer and member of the activist group We Can't Consent To This, which campaigns against the 'rough sex' defence in cases where women die and the accused, to date all male, claims she enthusiastically participated. Also known as the '50 Shades of Grey' defence, after the popular book and film, this has been used in court to justify the killing of a woman simply 'because she consented' to sex.

In the last five years, of nineteen homicide cases in which men killed women and used a defence of 'rough sex', nine defendants avoided a murder conviction. In two-thirds of those homicide cases, the women were killed by strangulation. Research published in 2019 showed that 38 per cent of UK women under forty have experienced non-consensual strangulation, gagging, spitting or slapping during sex; to put this in context in 1997 there were 115 such cases.

Between 1996 and 2016 there has been a tenfold increase in the use of this defence in the UK and, in every case, the defendant has been male, often with a substantial domestic abuse history or other convictions for serious violence against women, like rape, kidnap or homicide.

However, at the time of writing, We Can't Consent To This is celebrating a victory: changes to the 2020 Domestic Abuse Bill included a clear direction that the defence be abolished.

Alongside the feminist Labour MP and Attorney General Harriet Harman, in 2009 JfW also successfully campaigned for the abolition of that partial defence which JfW dubbed the 'nagging and shagging' defence due to the fact that so many men that killed their female partners claimed that he had been driven mad by her 'nagging' or that she had taunted him about having affairs with other men.

Profiting from abuse

Porn is a significant factor in shifting sexual norms. Erotic asphyxiation used to be regarded as a niche and risky sexual practice, enjoyed by a tiny community of sadomasochists who were overwhelmingly men. Now it has become mainstream to the point that magazines aimed at young women publish articles on how to be safely choked during sex, and tips for anal sex.

During 2019, there were twenty-three billion visits to the website Pornhub, which equates to a collective forty billion centuries of porn being viewed. Every minute, 11,082 hours of hardcore porn is being watched. That's 664,920 hours of content being consumed every hour, and 15,958,080 hours of pornographic videos being consumed every single day. The annual revenue from the porn industry has been estimated at $90 billion. To put that in context, the Hollywood film industry 'only' makes around $10 billion a year.

Progressives who defend pornography often miss the fact that the porn trade profits from the real-life abuse and degradation of some of the most disenfranchised women and girls.

When Rose Kalemba was fourteen, she was brutally raped by two men while a third man filmed the assault. The film ended up on Pornhub, entitled *Passed Out Teen* and *Teen Getting Destroyed*. Kalemba, now twenty-six, only discovered this when she saw school friends sharing the link on social media. Despite contacting Pornhub numerous times, begging them to take down the footage and explaining it was a recording of a sexual assault, she was ignored by the website until she threatened them with legal action. The footage was suddenly removed. Yet the day after Kalemba's story was published in a magazine and shared on social media, 'Passed Out Teen' and 'Teen Getting Destroyed' were both trending on Pornhub as search terms.

I ask what she thinks is going to change things for women. 'Radical feminism is the only way because it's real feminism,' she says. 'Women have been duped for so many years by liberal feminism, which celebrates abuse and degradation as empowering. It has to stop.'

In 2014, Israel became the first country to ban revenge porn in a bid to prevent the distribution of some pornographic content over the internet. The law, which targets sexually explicit media posted without the depicted person's knowledge or consent, also covers content shared on social media. It stipulates that those found guilty of posting such content will be prosecuted as sex offenders and that the offence is punishable by up to five years in prison. But to date, the young Israeli men accused of filming Emily in Ayia Napa have faced no consequences for doing exactly that.

But then the UK is hardly a good example of female-friendly legislation or application of the law. In April 2019, Justice Hayden provoked outrage from feminists when he told a court that it is a fundamental human right that a man should be able to have sex with his wife.

At the hearing Hayden said: 'I cannot think of any more obviously fundamental human right than the right of a man to have sex with his wife and the right of the state to monitor that. I think he is entitled to have it properly argued.' Hayden, a senior judge, made the comment in a case in which social services officials asked the court to determine whether a man should be prevented from having sex with his learning-disabled wife. Officials responsible for the woman's care had told the court there was evidence that her mental health had deteriorated to such an extent that she no longer had the capacity to consent to sex.

Two years later, in April 2021, Judge Hayden ruled that it is lawful for carers to assist their clients in paying for sex in particular circumstances. The case was brought on behalf of a twenty-seven-year-old mentally disabled man who was described as wishing to 'fulfil a natural desire'. The court heard that the man would 'probably never find a girlfriend' but he nevertheless wanted to experience sex, and had asked his carers if they could find him a prostituted woman (described in court as a 'sex worker') who would be paid to have sex with him. The idea that having sex is a human right, at least for men, is indicative of the ingrained sense of entitlement felt and expressed by men of all stripes.

We can't consent to this

Sadly, the well-publicised #MeToo movement appears to have made little difference when it comes to men's attitudes towards sex and the apparent 'moral grey area' of 'I thought she was enjoying it' – i.e. rape. Again, this is undoubtedly due to the prevalence of increasingly violent pornography. Whereas in the 1970s and 1980s men sexually assaulted women because they wanted to and because they could get away with it, now men have to dress up their coercion and frame it as 'sex-positive' experimentation in an effort to avoid the cognitive dissonance of apparently believing that 'consent matters' while proceeding on the basis that 'no' means 'convince me'.

For Tom Farr, a legal scholar who writes about and campaigns against male violence, a combination of widespread porn use alongside the power imbalance between men and women has 'acted as a fertiliser to male entitlement'. He says: 'Consent is no longer brushed under the rug but, thanks to feminism, placed at front and centre, so men have had to find a new way around that.'

Farr is right. By using violent, coercive porn as the yardstick for what sex should look like, coupled with the social propagation of 'anything should go in the name of progressive-ness', it has suddenly become much easier for men to say 'it wasn't rape because it was just experimentation'. It's easier to move the goalposts than pretend they don't exist.

The men's rights movement

It is blindingly obvious that feminism has not yet achieved its goals. We can see this in the levels of misogyny towards women and girls and the impunity with which men commit rape and domestic abuse. However much others might like us to set our sights so low that we would be grateful for a few scraps of the table – and put up with gross sexism on a daily basis – there is clearly still a huge amount of work to do before women are truly liberated. While the arguments of old were that we had been 'given' the vote; that we had, at least officially, equal pay for equal work; and that abortion was decriminalised, the scale and prevalence of male violence continues to speak volumes.

Men's rights activists have gained traction. They are no longer leaping from tall buildings wearing superhero costumes, as Fathers 4 Justice member Jason Hatch did when he scaled the walls of Buckingham Palace dressed as Batman to protest child custody policy in 2004. Instead, they are sitting at the table with legislators and politicians. These men, and a number of female supporters, are not like the blatantly misogynistic men of old, who would write books and newspaper columns denouncing feminism as being 'anti-men' and led by ugly lesbians with a (double-headed) axe to grind. Instead they are wolves in sheep's clothing.

These men form organisations with a remit to support male victims of female violence but which are in fact pressure groups with an aim to discredit the claims of anti-male-violence feminists regarding the prevalence of domestic violence and sexual assault. These men's rights activists continue to insist that 'women make it up', whether about rape or other forms of male violence, and to position themselves as the victims.

In February 2005, the last time I spoke to Andrea Dworkin prior to her death two months later, I asked how she coped with hearing endless stories about the abuse and degradation of women. She replied, 'If I give up now, younger generations of women will be told that porn is good for them and they will believe it.' Seventeen years later, it is horribly clear that her prediction came true. But as bleak as things seem to be right now, young women are fighting back.

The resurgence of feminist activism, in particular in relation to campaigns against male violence, is a response to the unbridled misogyny on both the left and the right. 'Cancel' culture, aimed at us 'disobedient bitches' daring to challenge the faux feminism promoted by male and female anti-feminists, shows how dangerous and disruptive to the patriarchal status quo we are. Our work is far from done while sites like Pornhub promote rape as entertainment, and lesbians are told to 'suck my dick' for refusing to capitulate to bullies.

Woman-hating has been dressed up as progressive politics. The feminists are stripping the mannequin bare.

Chapter 2

Shooting the Messenger:
How Feminists Are Blamed for the
Victimisation of Women

'The whole drive and dream of feminism is to no
longer be a victim. The ridiculous idea [that feminism
promotes victimhood] is probably just an effort to get
women to shut up about injustice.'

Gloria Steinem

It might surprise some to know that in 1994 I worked in a
police station in London, joining forces with macho coppers
in the fight against domestic violence. I was one of the civilian
advocates that would accompany police each time they were
called to a report of 'a domestic' in order that police could focus
on arresting the perpetrator whilst the advocate offered support
and information to the victim.

My first call-out was to Louise*, aged nineteen, who had just
given birth. Louise's boyfriend had beaten her as she held the
baby. Whilst the police searched the neighbourhood for him,
Louise told me about how he enjoyed kicking the backs of her
shins as she wheeled the baby in the pram. She showed me the
marks where he'd stubbed out his cigarettes on her arms.

The police returned, without the perpetrator, and started questioning Louise about the mess in the flat, suggesting that he had 'lost it' with her because he was 'living in chaos'. They were referring to unwashed dishes and a crying baby. Louise decided not to press charges, and I returned to the station feeling angry and worried for her safety.

There was one police officer based in the Domestic Violence Unit that would return from domestic abuse visits telling us it was, 'six of one and half-a-dozen of the other'. Most of the 999 calls came from a large social housing estate in a particularly run-down area, and the police officers judged the women harshly, commenting on how much they drank, smoked and swore. The behaviour of the violent men was rarely referred to, and they were rarely arrested.

Some years later, in 2003, I spent several weeks at the Old Bailey criminal court in London observing rape trials for a research project.

The police officers dealing with rape cases in London at the time were part of a gold-standard crack team, and were specially trained in the law, investigating techniques, interviewing skills and empathy for complainants.

One case was particularly harrowing: a fifteen-year-old girl named Carla* had gone home with a twenty-five-year-old man to his flat on the promise of a second-hand PlayStation. Once in the flat, the girl was raped anally, orally and vaginally whilst being filmed by the perpetrator. The footage of her rape was submitted for evidence, and we got to see it in the court. I was struggling not to cry, as were many of the jury, and the judge, sensing the mood of the court, ordered a short recess.

I stood outside the court trying to gain my composure and behind me came two male officers. One of them said to the other of the complainant, 'What a fucking idiot, what did she expect, going back home with a grown man?' The other officer affected a creepy voice, seemingly imitating the perpetrator, 'Why don't you come back and see my puppies, little girl?'

I complained to the court usher, and he told me that police officers often have 'gallows humour' in order to 'cope' with the job.

Almost two decades later, in 2021, I am in Birmingham Crown Court for the murder trial of Emma-Jayne Magson, a young woman who had killed her abusive boyfriend after months of violence. Magson was convicted of murder despite the court being provided with ample evidence of his abuse, including a violent attack in the street hours before she killed him which was captured on CCTV.

In sentencing Magson, the judge said he did not believe she showed any remorse for taking a life. Even prison officers testify to her constantly talking about how she feels shame and regret. As Magson has since said, 'It's terrible to hurt someone. I would never fight back again.'

I have lost count of the times I have directly witnessed victim blaming, and my heart breaks at the tragic consequences of pointing the finger at abused women and defending violent men.

Louise*, the young woman I visited with the police in 1994, was killed by her boyfriend less than a year after we met. I still dream of her to this day.

The defendant in Clara*'s case was acquitted of rape. I later learned through press reports that he has since appeared in court again for the rape of a teenager and was acquitted a second time.

During my time as a feminist I have been both physically and sexually assaulted by men, and I was scared. Male violence terrifies me, which is why I fight to end it. The feminists I campaign alongside give me the courage to do it.

I have long been told that feminists create fear in women, putting the idea in their heads that men are dangerous predators. We apparently scare other women into imagining men permanently crouched in alleyways waiting to commit acts of rape and murder. Feminists, therefore, are the ones who curtail women's lives and prevent them from living as free and equal citizens. Rapists and murderers apparently play no part in that.

Within this narrative, those labelled 'victim feminists' spend disproportionate amounts of time focusing on rape, domestic violence and femicide because they believe that men are innately bad and that women are faint-hearted weaklings in desperate need of a 'trigger warning' about every single thing.

The notion that feminists are to blame for making women scared of men and exaggerating male violence is not surprising. Women are often blamed for male violence anyway, so blaming feminists for drawing attention to it makes sense within that context.

Yet there are irrefutable statistics about violence against women and girls. The hardest facts and figures come out of the mortuaries and are buried in graves around the world. Research by the United Nations Office for Drugs and Crime and the feminist NGO Femicide Watch found that at least eighty-seven thousand women worldwide were killed by men in 2019.

Jessica Taylor, author of *Why Women Are Blamed For Everything: Exploring the Victim Blaming of Women Subjected to Violence* (2020) and the founder of the Victim Focus campaign, believes that women can only demand justice for male violence if it is acknowledged that we are victimised by it. To deny that status makes it possible for the perpetrators and wider society to ignore the abuser and put the blame squarely on the shoulders of those who have been harmed.

'Girls are blamed for being abused into prostitution,' she says. 'Women are blamed for rape. We are blamed for things men do to us. What that means is a double punishment and a complete free rein for male abusers.'

When I first became active in the women's liberation movement in the late 1970s, those accusing us of practising 'victim feminism' – a term that had been in use since the previous decade – were blatant anti-feminists: they were men's rights activists who wanted to deny the prevalence of male violence. But since then, a new wave of feminists has couched the meaning of the victim feminism slur in 'progressive' language, using the insult because they have bought in to the idea that it's liberating.

'Victim feminism' has now been popularised by women who want to distance themselves from feminism yet claim to be feminists in order to gain authority on the topic. Katie Roiphe used the term in her 1993 essay 'The Morning After: Sex, Fear, and Feminism on Campus' when she said that feminism 'transforms perfectly stable women into hysterical, sobbing victims'.

But campaigning against male violence is at the heart of all feminism – and it always has been.

* * *

Even in the first wave of feminism (also known as the Suffrage movement) when women were not only campaigning for the vote but also, among other things, for employment rights, for marriage rights and so on, they were also lobbying against the barbaric violence imposed on women who were forced into institutions such as the workhouse or the lock hospital, as well as domestic violence.

Early feminists formed consciousness-raising groups to talk about their collective experiences of male violence, abuse and harassment and the women's liberation movement was founded in order to resist this – by documenting the extent of male violence and abuse – and to liberate women from it through orchestrated campaigns and other methods.

It was very difficult for many heterosexual women to accept what feminists were saying about the nature and prevalence of male violence. Many refused to believe it was about men as a sex class as opposed to random individuals committing crimes, and because of the level of denial within society, they turned their anger not on abusive men but on feminists, resenting them for exposing the extent of male violence and blaming them for creating a culture of fear as well as a moral panic about child sexual abuse, rape and domestic violence, while men's rights activists hit back, saying that they were also victims.

Today feminists are still blamed for frightening women into believing that they are at risk of male violence, and this is because women are blamed for everything and feminists are blamed doubly. Feminists are hated because women are hated. This sounds harsh, and for heterosexual women it is particularly unforgiving. After all, there are many good men and countless examples of happy heterosexual relationships that seem to contradict this. But no society would permit what happens to women and girls if, at some level, it didn't have contempt for us.

Fighting back

Feminists demand that male violence against women and girls be taken seriously. We demand that men are held accountable when they commit rape and other forms of sex-based atrocities. To this end, countless women and girls who have endured the most extreme acts of male violence are bravely using their experiences to campaign for justice.

When Rachel Williams was shot by her ex-husband in 2011, she had been expecting it. Darren Williams' violence had been extreme, involving beating his wife when she was seven months pregnant and strangling her until her lips turned blue. After Rachel finally managed to leave him, he stalked and threatened her, and she feared he would murder her. This is nothing unusual: domestic violence perpetrators often live out the cliché of 'if I can't have you, nobody can' and approximately half of all women who die at the hands of violent ex- or current partners do so when they leave or attempt to leave.

Family annihilation sprees so often see the violent man who can no longer control his victim killing his wife or partner, and on some occasions the children, before killing himself, and this was no exception. If the two gunshots that Darren had fired at a fleeing Rachel had hit her in the stomach as he intended, rather than her leg, she would now be dead. Shortly afterwards, he was found hanging in the woods. And while he did not also murder his children, six weeks after the shooting, Rachel's sixteen-year-old son Jack took his own life.

On the anniversary of Jack's death in 2019, Rachel shared a photo of his cremation file on social media to show 'the reality of domestic abuse and violence', which doesn't just affect the adults involved but the whole family. She has organised a number of successful petitions as well as an annual Stand Up to Domestic Violence conference and works tirelessly to raise awareness as well as to try to bring this crime to an end. Almost losing her own life and enduring the pain of her son's death galvanised Rachel into campaigning to end male violence. Who victimised Rachel? Who frightened her? It certainly wasn't feminists.

Rachel is just one example of a woman who came to feminism through experiencing and fighting back against male violence. Whether it's women escaping the sex trade and fighting to reveal the truth about prostitution; those targeted by men using revenge porn who have spoken out and brought a change in the law; rape victims who change the way we view sexual assault; or young women resisting forced marriage and FGM while challenging white liberals on harmful cultural practices, these women are the backbone of the women's liberation movement.

The power of feminism

In July 2016, the Wolfpack (so called because the victim described the rapists as acting 'like a pack of wolves') gang rape case in Spain brought feminists out onto the streets in force.

The police compiled a two-hundred-page report that described the woman's state as 'passive and neutral' (possibly due to her being intoxicated and semi-conscious), meaning that, because there was no 'violence or intimidation', the perpetrators were not guilty of sexual assault. However, they were still found guilty of sexual abuse, which doesn't require violence or intimidation. As an aside, the court rejected video evidence of the same men sitting in a van with a different unconscious twenty-one-year-old, talking about 'fucking Sleeping Beauty'.

Defence lawyers had argued that the gang had not subjected the victim to 'sexual aggression'. But when the case reached the Supreme Court, the ruling was overturned because it was found that the woman was 'overcome by fear'. Finally, in June 2019, the men were convicted of rape and each sentenced to fifteen years in prison.

The feminist campaign around the Wolfpack case led to the numbers of women calling themselves feminists *and* reports of rape increasing across Spain. That is the power of feminism: to join forces as a collective movement to protest against male violence and the state failures in relation to it, and to support the victims.

The female backlash against feminism

The backlash against the feminist response to this case came largely from men but also some women – 'power feminists' – who fight more for the 'right' of women to say 'yes' to the consumption of pornography and harmful sexual practices such as BDSM than the right to say 'no' to men.

Power feminism took root in the 1990s. The concept was developed by women such as Naomi Wolf, Katie Roiphe and Camille Paglia to counter what they saw as the feebleness of anti-male-violence (or what they termed 'victim') feminists for continuing to point to the perpetrators as being responsible for the crimes they committed.

Power feminism adheres to the principle that rather than drawing the attention of women to our oppression, we should encourage them into the movement by emphasising women's potential and resilience. Victim feminism, according to Wolf in *Fire with Fire: The New Female Power and How It Will Change the 21st Century* (1993) simply casts women as 'beleaguered, fragile, intuitive angels'.

Paglia backs this up. 'These women passing out with terror every time a man compliments their breasts makes a mockery of feminism,' she tells me over Skype, adding, 'I think like a man, I don't know how I can do that, but I can. I refuse to be a victim, like so many soft-assed women.'

One way that 'power feminism' has influenced young women in particular is when it comes to heterosexual sexual practices favoured by porn-sick men. The 'I'm not a victim' mantra has become so commonplace among young women that they are being sold a version of sexual liberation that is merely eroticised sexual violence. To protest this brings about accusations of victimhood.

The latest addition to the LGBTQQIA+ is K for 'kink'. Much of what is called kink is really BDSM (bondage, discipline, sadomasochism), with the majority of heterosexual men who practise BDSM taking on the role of the sadist.

Strangulation is extremely popular among male BDSMers. In a recent animation-style 'safety guide' aimed at young women involved in BDSM, the strangler was advised to watch the face of the person he is strangling in case it goes a puce colour, and to make sure that any bloodshot marks in the eyes are given time to heal before resuming the choking. Of course, if a person wishes to seek sexual pleasure from being throttled, who am I to interfere? A good liberal response would be to repeat the clichéd mantra, 'What happens between consenting adults in the bedroom …'

In February 2021, *Cosmopolitan* ran a story pegged on the case of Armie Hammer, an actor who is alleged to have sent several messages to a number of women in which he expressed his penchant for cannibalism. In one message it is alleged that Hammer told the recipient he wanted to, 'bite pieces off' her and eat her heart. Another reads: 'I am 100% a cannibal. I want to eat you. F---. That's scary to admit. I've never admitted that before.'

Hammer denies the allegations, claiming the messages have not been verified. But cannibalism – the act of eating a fellow human – is described by the 'sex positive' crew as a 'kink'.

Cosmopolitan, whose main target audience is females between the ages of eighteen and thirty-five, appears to be fond of promoting such practices. For example, its 2021 guide to anal sex for beginners ('you need *a lot* of lube') rushed to reassure its readers that, 'Yes, There's a Safe Way to Have a Cannibalism Fetish.' I had assumed this was a bad taste piece from *The Onion*.

The immediate response to a critique of the 'all sex is good sex' narrative tends to be along the lines of 'You think women who disagree with you don't understand their own lives and desires,' and that I am accusing women who proport to enjoy harmful sexual practices as suffering from 'false consciousness'. But false consciousness exists.

Women tend to develop all sorts of strategies for coping with male violence and their own subordination, including eroticising it themselves. 'I got into BDSM,' says Kerry, a student in her early twenties, 'because I reckoned if I could "play out" the sexual abuse from childhood, I would be in control of it and it would stop the demons in my head. But all it did was reinforce how worthless I felt.'

These strategies include denial of the everyday threat and reality of male violence, justifying male behaviour, (and even as Catharine Mackinnon describes it, 'grateful complicity in exchange for survival'). Feminism offers instead a survival strategy of developing a sense of self and of self-respect, but living under the conditions of patriarchy makes that appear to be a more difficult option.

What does consent mean for women living in a world awash with misogyny? And how does this fit with the increased normalisation of strangulation?

Normalising sexual violence

The rise of the 'rough sex' defence is a clear indication of the increasing normalisation of sexual sadism and violence towards women. Fiona McKenzie from the feminist campaign group We Can't Consent to This tells me that in both fatal and non-fatal sexual and violent assaults on women, the use of the 'rough sex games gone wrong' defence is becoming more commonplace.

Of the women killed, half were in relationships with the men who killed them. Most of those men had a history of abuse. And many of these defendants had other convictions for serious violence – rape, murder, kidnap – of women.

The 2020 Femicide Census catalogued eight women killed in sexually sadistic homicides in 2018. Six of the eight male defendants used a 'rough sex' defence in order to plead the lesser charge of manslaughter.

Then there are those who object to feminists spoiling their fun by talking about male harassment and verbal abuse because *they like it*! Paris Lees is a trans woman who identifies as a feminist. Writing in *Vice* about a holiday in Ibiza, she said she was 'catcalled, sexually objectified and treated like a piece of meat by men the entire week. And it was absolutely awesome.' Lees was writing in opposition to an article by Laura Bates, founder of the Everyday Sexism project, on the prevalence of street harassment and the feminist campaign to eradicate it. According to Lees, the feminist objection to men harassing women in public is 'part of a culture that infantilises women and teaches them to be constantly afraid'.

Turning her analysis to class, she then suggests that a 'certain kind of middle-class woman' is particularly offended by catcalls: 'There's a sense of being sullied if an uncouth or lower-class kind of man – a white van man, for example – heckles.' These middle-class women apparently believe that 'all men are rapists-in-waiting and that all women are victims-in-waiting'.

For Lees, the working-class builder is the victim of classist bigotry from women. Which is neat. It follows the same logic that she has often espoused about trans women being the victim of 'cis-sexism' by natal women.

Like Lees, Ella Whelan, author of *What Women Want: Fun, Freedom And An End to Feminism* (2017), similarly adopts a class-war stance: 'If you have a feminist movement that says, "OMG, this guy looked at me/stood too near to me/I'm going to fall on the floor and die if someone pinches my bum", then you're doomed.' For Whelan, not all women are oppressed, and middle-class white women simply wish to make a career out of feminism: 'These women essentially ride on the backs of women who are genuinely suffering oppression.'

I am unsure how anti-male-violence feminists ride on the backs of genuinely oppressed women. I have never noticed what a lucrative business calling out rapists and perpetrators of domestic violence is. Additionally, what about the sexual harassment of working-class and migrant women?

In 2012, two female asylum seekers being held at Yarl's Wood Detention Centre spoke out about being sexually harassed and 'preyed upon' by SERCO guards. 'These women were incredibly brave to speak out,' says Harriet Wistrich, the feminist lawyer who represented the women. 'They did so in order to expose the scandal of male officers taking advantage of vulnerable women, despite the precariousness of their asylum status.'

Then there is Annie*, who I interviewed in 2013. Annie, a working-class young woman who suffers from mental ill health, first complained about Mike Hancock, a former Liberal Democrat MP, in early 2011. Annie approached Hancock in 2009 over problems with noisy neighbours and respite care for her son. She told him about her mental health problems (brought about by childhood sexual abuse) and that she had been diagnosed with a 'borderline personality disorder'. Over the following months Hancock began to see Annie regularly, to buy her gifts, including a teddy bear he named 'Mike', and once took her out to dinner at the House of Commons. Hancock would send Annie regular text messages, all of which she kept. Such as: 'Please give me a chance you never know my Princess xxx' and '. . . you are special and sexy to me'.

Annie did not want a sexual relationship and felt confused that such a powerful man had shown an interest in her. The following summer Annie broke down and told her family support worker about Hancock's behaviour, who gave her permission to report him to the police. 'I made a statement to police but something about their response left me wondering if anything would be done about him,' she told me. 'Hancock is such a powerful man after all.'

After a five-year campaign, Hancock issued a public apology, 'I understand that you felt degraded. I did not treat you with sufficient respect. I made you feel deeply uncomfortable and discriminated against . . . As a political representative, there is a significant power differential with any constituent seeking help and particularly with your vulnerability of which I was aware.'

Similarly, look at the feminist influence within the trades union movement that worked so hard to include an end to sexual harassment as part of workers' rights. The likes of Paris Lees may well enjoy 'being treated like a piece of meat', but the fact is that many women have no choice in the matter.

Women-only space

The concept of safe spaces came about for this very reason. It is rooted in early second-wave feminism when it was recognised that there was a need for protected places away from male interference in which women could explore issues specific to them, and as refuges to escape danger.

The concept of safe space extended to mental space. While feminists working to end male violence did recognise women's right to choose not to engage with extreme porn, I and many others thought it important to know exactly what we were objecting to. Indeed, my argument was always that for feminists to effectively argue and campaign against pornography it was necessary to have seen it and to that end, a number of us travelled the UK in the late 1980s and early 1990s to show what we called the 'porn slide show', which we screened at women-only events. Even though all the attendees had signed up to the meeting in the full knowledge of what they would be seeing, some still argued that they should be protected from viewing images of women being tortured in front of a camera – despite the fact that this material was all around us. And those same arguments are prevalent today, even though, with the growth of the internet, it's increasingly readily available.

The pornography I have looked at, including snuff movies (where women are gravely injured and/or murdered in reality), has taken its toll. I have had nightmares about women being gang raped, and terrible flashbacks as I recounted some of the stories told to me by women who endured the worst of sexual abuse.

Despite this, I consider 'trigger warnings' – which are inserted before almost any statement about almost any topic (interestingly except, in the main, misogyny) to protect students from learning about issues that may cause them distress – to be both ridiculous and a perversion of the original concept of safe spaces.

Harvard law lecturer Jeannie Suk wrote in her 2014 article 'The Trouble with Teaching Rape Law', that student groups are demanding that certain 'upsetting details' contained in case law documents are left out of lectures in case they cause distress to rape survivors. Yet is it not rank hypocrisy that some of the very same critics of 'victim feminism' support the thin-skinned, easily offended, middle-class whingers who cannot even bear to read or hear about sexual violence?

More recently, terms such as 'triggering' and 'safe spaces' have been co-opted by those claiming to be traumatised by certain ideas and ideologies rather than those who have first-hand lived experiences of these issues.

In 2018 I was invited to an American university to debate, alongside a men's rights activist, whether feminism had 'gone too far'. The man I was debating with had spoken out about how he believed abortion should be criminalised and rape decriminalised, with an exemption for stranger attacks by masked marauders. Astonishingly, the pickets on campus focused on me, not him. The LGBTQQIA+ caucus objected to my presence on the basis that I was so transphobic I would trigger suicidal ideation of transgender students and cause literal harm.

Of course, as with similar incidents, the caucus did their very best to have me disinvited from the event. When that failed, the university did the next best thing: on the opposite side of the campus to where I was speaking, one of the teaching rooms was turned into a therapy hub. There were trained counsellors on site, the room was littered with soft toys, and there were even a couple of dogs and cats brought along for non-judgemental cuddling. I was told by someone who had popped in to observe that the walls were strewn with 'affirmative statements' such as 'trans women are women' and 'non-binary identities are valid'.

Rebranding victimhood

The uses and misuses of the victim narrative are far-reaching and extend into all aspects of the feminist cause.

This narrative is increasingly being used by the 'sex workers' rights' movement to discredit feminists campaigning to end violence against women; according to organisations such as the English Collective of Prostitutes, the International Union of Sex Workers and others, women involved in prostitution are not abused or exploited by the pimps and the punters, but by the feminists who consider prostitution to be harmful. These organisations argue that if only the entire sex trade, including pimping, brothel-owning and paying for sex, was decriminalised – and feminists such as myself stopped going on about the violence and abuse within it – then everything would be hunky-dory.

It is interesting to note that during the 1980s and 1990s, when feminists in the UK began to openly debate the issue of prostitution and its harms to women, those with no direct experience of the sex trade were told to shut up and let the women with the experience speak. Which would have been fine, except the women speaking tended to be those at the pimping end of prostitution as opposed to those being exploited.

Later in the 1990s, as sex-trade survivors began to speak out and form their own campaign groups, the response was to suggest that they were lying, exaggerating or simply mad. This is perfectly illustrated by the case of Rachel Moran, an Irish sex-trade survivor and author of the bestselling memoir *Paid For: My Journey through Prostitution* (2013). Moran knew that not everybody would be happy that she had laid bare the realities of sexual exploitation. Pimps, brothel owners and punters would certainly not be pleased that she had lifted the lid on the world's oldest form of oppression of women. What she could never have imagined was having to sue another woman for defamation.

Gaye Dalton, who was also involved in prostitution in Dublin's southside red-light district, one of the spots where

Moran was bought and sold, has repeatedly alleged that Moran fabricated her life history and had never even been in prostitution. These extraordinary claims were ruled as 'untrue, offensive and defamatory' by a judge in Dublin's Circuit Court in November 2019, and Dalton was legally restricted from repeating them.

Impunity for violent men?

Another thing 'victim feminists' are accused of is using victimhood in order to demand support from the state, namely the criminal justice system. 'Carceral' is commonly used to discredit those of us who wish to see men who pay for sex criminalised, and also as a critique of anyone who wants to keep criminal penalties on domestic violence.

The thrust of the accusation is that those of us that want consequences for men who rape and otherwise abuse women are unconcerned with the fact that the prison system is a problem in general, and more specifically that people of colour and other marginalised and disenfranchised communities are more likely to be given custodial sentences and suffer additional harm, including death in custody, during their sentences. What the accusers seem less concerned about is the fact that the vast majority of those incarcerated in women's prisons have been victims of sexual and other forms of violence committed by men who have rarely been held to account.

Claire Heuchan, co-author of *What Is Race? Who Are Racists? Why Does Skin Colour Matter? And Other Big Questions* (2018) says that while she acknowledges that prison abolitionist feminists raise serious questions about the criminal justice system and the inequalities underpinning it, they have so far failed to provide a satisfying answer about what should happen to the men who kill, rape, stalk and abuse women.

'I am conscious that race and class both play a big role in determining who is criminalised and how,' says Heuchan. 'Angela Davis' book *Freedom Is a Constant Struggle* is amazing in a lot of ways. But she never addresses that the majority of female prisoners have experienced some form of male violence.'

I have been called a carceral feminist on numerous occasions, despite the fact that I have spent more than three decades campaigning against unnecessary prison sentences, am a founder of a law reform organisation, and have led numerous campaigns to free abused women from life sentences for killing violent men.

The term 'carceral' was originally used by black American prison abolitionists to highlight the over-criminalisation of black men in the USA, but is now used by the likes of Professor Alison Phipps, who is white, to mean women who support campaigns like #MeToo or lobby for dangerous sexual predators to spend time in prison. It is only ever used as an insult; a clue to this is that there are *no* self-identified 'carceral feminists' just as there are no self-identified 'TERFs' (although some feminists now choose to use the term ironically and in humour).

Phipps' book *Me, Not You: The Trouble with Mainstream Feminism* (2020) is peppered with 'carceral' accusations against anti-male-violence feminists, and Molly Smith and Juno Mac, in their book *Revolting Prostitutes* (2018), claim that feminists working to end demand for prostitution are colluding with the state to control poor, migrant workers.

US-based academic Chloe Taylor has written several critiques of carceral feminism. In a 2009 paper entitled 'Foucault,

Feminism, and Sex Crimes', she appears to lay the blame for women's fear of male violence not just on us feminists but also on 'women-run rape crisis centres'.

Taylor argues that these, together with women-only self-defence classes, reinforce the notion that male sexuality is dangerous and women's bodies are sexually vulnerable. Therefore, women-only responses to male sexual violence 'reinscribe the construction of an adversarial and biologically grounded male/female dichotomy rather than challenging it. It is these constructions, I suggest, that are the cause of rape.'

Taylor's attempt at a defence of Michel Foucault is a valiant one. He was a libertarian who argued that statutory rape should no longer be a crime; that sex between adults and children was unproblematic; and that rape was no more serious than a punch in the face. Taylor's conclusion is also valiant: she states that feminists should prioritise changing the social context in which sexual violence occurs rather than focusing on criminal justice responses. Perhaps if she understood anti-male-violence feminism better she would realise we have been doing both at the same time.

In another paper, 'Anti-Carceral Feminism and Sexual Assault – A Defence' (2018), Taylor lays out her position very clearly on those who call for criminal justice sanctions as a response to men's sexual violence towards women. Rightly pointing out the prevalence of sexual assault and rape within prisons, she appears to be arguing for an amnesty on rapists lest they are faced with sexual violence themselves: 'Anyone concerned with preventing sexual crimes such as rape should be engaged not so much in putting sex offenders in prisons as in keeping them out of prisons, since prison is one of the most likely places for rape to occur and for a culture of rape to be normalised.'

But, as Pragna Patel, one of the founders of the feminist group Southall Black Sisters says: 'Incarceration has to remain an option for those seeking accountability and protection in the absence of anything better.'

Feminists who campaign to end male violence do not wish to see the perpetrators subjected to sexual assault themselves. There have rarely, if ever, been vigilante groups comprised of such feminists, despite the fact that male violence is an everyday occurrence and can have terrible consequences for the victims and the wider community. These feminists support measures that will result in men being deterred from committing such violent acts in a culture in which there is impunity for men who target women and children.

Punishing women, protecting men

For me, prison is less about punishment and more about protecting women from violent men who often reoffend. It should be possible to challenge the race and class hierarchies upheld by the criminal justice system without putting women from all backgrounds at greater risk of male violence.

In 2009, I attended the national Police Vice Conference that dealt with issues from child abuse images online to international sex-trafficking rings. A handful of civilians was invited every year, and I was asked to speak about a proposed change to the law that would effectively criminalise those who pay for sex. A cohort of pro-prostitution academics and harm-minimisation service providers also attended, but they were presenting research that they argued showed that barely any women in the indoor sex trade in the UK had been trafficked or otherwise coerced into prostitution. Therefore, they were arguing that the men who pay for sex are merely one half of a business transaction and that the law should not interfere in that business.

I approached one of the academics and asked if she would consider speaking to her colleagues who believed that prostitution is 'work', to ask if they would join a coalition with abolitionists to demand that any person selling sex be decriminalised and have all previous criminal records relating to prostitution wiped. The academics agreed and we put forward a plan that we presented to the most senior police officers in the country, and a proposal to change the law, which a number of them supported.

Years later, having chewed over the idea since 1999 and after conversations with sex-trade survivors with criminal records, a number of feminist lawyers and activists took a case to court which led to a change in the law. As a result of the judicial review, anyone who accrued a criminal record for street soliciting offences while below the age of eighteen would no longer have to disclose the criminal record when going for jobs or volunteer positions.

It's interesting that the sex-trade abolitionist feminists, so often accused of being 'carceral', rather than the pro-prostitution lobbyists, were the ones to succeed in effectively decriminalising large numbers of formerly prostituted women.

Victim v survivor

One of the great achievements of anti-male-violence feminism is that we have helped to educate the wider public about the widescale sexual and physical violence and abuse perpetrated by men against women and girls. But even so, when we talk about the sheer extent of male violence, we can be accused of practising victim feminism as an attempt to shut us up.

As a progressive movement, feminism has been keen to reject this status and instead to highlight our strong resistance to oppression. Many of us are cynical about the victims' rights movement (the victim of crime demanding the status of an interested party with recognised rights in the justice system) but often the women involved in such a movement are fighting to get justice, not to wallow in victimhood. The status of victim can dignify them. It means they are taken seriously by state agencies in wider society. '[Victim is] a true word,' wrote Andrea Dworkin. 'If you were raped, you were victimised. You damned well were. You were a victim . . . And if it happens to you systematically because you are born a woman, it means that you live in a political system that uses pain and humiliation to control and to hurt you.'

When we refer to the victims of male violence as 'survivors', it is a value-laden term and can have an impact and consequences for victims. These women are expected to be heroic, to not just survive but to thrive, and to represent other women who have endured similar ordeals. They are called brave and treated as though they are somehow special because of what they have been through. Obviously, it takes courage to stand up in a room full of people or to go in front of the TV cameras and speak about being raped or sexually abused as a child. It takes guts to relive the horrors of the sex trade from personal experience, bearing in mind the stigma is firmly on the woman rather than the punter. But the glorification of survivors can have the effect of stigmatising some victims and can lead to a presumption of iron will among those who speak out.

#MeToo

In 2017, there were a few months of heightened media interest in feminist issues thanks to the surge in women sharing stories of their sexual assaults via the hashtag #MeToo and in response to a number of high-profile women publicising their assaults by well-known and powerful men. But the #MeToo movement was nothing new. It was started in 2006 by Tarana Burke, an African American activist, as a way to process the sexual abuse she had experienced and to support girls going through the same. Burke has said that as a child she didn't have any resources and she wanted other girls to have access to the support she didn't have. In 2017, the phrase became a hashtag promoted by high-profile female actors such as Rose McGowan and Alyssa Milano, who were victims of the prolific sexual predator Harvey Weinstein. Milano tweeted: 'If you've been sexually harassed or assaulted write "me too" as a reply to this tweet.' Hundreds of thousands of women did just that.

Despite the creation of laws and policies designed to protect women from such violence and abuse, often they are poorly implemented by the police and other criminal justice agencies. Things today appear to be every bit as bad as – or much worse than – during the 1980s and 1990s, which is why feminists continue to develop new campaign tactics, and younger women dare to come forward and campaign against the current and insidious forms of misogyny.

As the #MeToo stories of Hollywood actors and powerful men shifted from social media to mainstream media, women's control of their own stories became limited and depoliticised. The fact that speaking out is removed from the context of feminism allows for the feminist story of sexual harassment and violence in the context of male violence and supremacy to be rewritten or misunderstood as a story about feminist in-fighting. While personal silences are broken, political silences can be reinforced because the backlash from the misogynists may scare into silence those who want to be speaking out.

As a key aim of feminism is to end the victimisation of women and girls and we seek to encourage women everywhere to speak out about what is done to us, the stigma and shame when we are raped and abused has to be shifted firmly onto the men that commit these acts, and the men who refuse to speak out against them. Feminism is about giving women the strength and courage to say no, the most important word in the feminist dictionary. There is no shame in shouting as loud as we can about what men do to us, and we must refuse to be silent.

Chapter 3

Women's Liberation or Bust: Why Equality Is Not Enough

'Women who want to be equal with men lack ambition.'
Marilyn Monroe

A Man's Right to Be Right

On the train from London to Durham in 2014, I was trying to prepare my fifteen-minute opening speech for an event at the University of Durham Debating Society. Scratching my head at the title of the debate – 'This House believes feminists are all too often sexists in disguise' – I wondered how I might argue against such a ludicrous proposition. Suddenly, as the train passed Peterborough, I knew exactly what my opponent, men's rights anti-feminist lobbyist Mike Buchanan, would say. Something along the well-worn path of, 'Why should women get special treatment? Equality is for everyone.'

Mike Buchanan has been very vocal about his hatred of feminists. He once argued that 'hatchet-faced' women are drawn to feminism 'like moths to a flame', because they are jealous of women whom men find attractive.

Buchanan has also claimed that women are more violent than men, that they are taught to 'cry rape', and that those fighting for equality with men are encouraging a 'hostile anti-male culture'.

Clearly, I was looking forward to sparring with him.

Unsurprisingly, the event got off to a lively start. Buchanan opened with the argument that men are 'so much' worse off than women in almost every way before switching to the example of Justice for Women, the organisation I co-founded in 1991:

'Let's imagine that someone emailed you a link to the website of a campaigning organisation called "Justice for Men" ... sounds innocuous, doesn't it? You click on the link, and beneath a sinister logo you see the strapline, "Women, men and murder". You then read this, on the first line of the home page:

"Justice for Men was established as a campaigning organisation that supports and advocates on behalf of men who have fought back against or killed violent female partners."

'I find the idea of an organisation supporting and advocating for men who have fought back against or killed their female partners repellent, and an example of extreme sexism. If any of you in the audience wouldn't find such an organisation repellent and sexist, would you please put up your hands now?'

In an audience of over three hundred people, almost all university students, not one hand was raised.

'Thank you. There is, however, no campaigning organisation called Justice for Men. But there is one called "Justice for Women", and it was co-founded many years ago by Julie Bindel.'

There is, in fact, an organisation called 'Justice for Men' – or rather, to give it its full glorious title, Justice for Men and Boys (and the women who love them), and, what's more, Buchanan is its founder.

Buchanan was extremely proud of himself. He believed he had successfully highlighted how outrageously sexist feminists are. After all, if we support women who kill men, then it is perfectly reasonable to support men who kill women.

Without context, Buchanan's argument may seem reasonable to a small number of people who conflate fairness with 'sameness'; but women and men do not have the same experience. The vast majority of women who die at the hands of former and current partners have suffered ongoing domestic violence at the hands of the perpetrator, whereas the relatively few women who kill do so in response to violence from the deceased.

The day I debated Buchanan and was told that feminism is sexist, unfair and discriminatory towards men, the news was full of reports on male violence towards women and girls. For example, a fourteen-year-old girl was in critical condition after being raped and left for dead by a fifteen-year-old boy.

James Simister was in court charged with the murder of his wife Deborah whom he had repeatedly stabbed in the neck as she prepared to leave him. The defence barrister described the relationship as 'volatile' – but the violence was all directed one way.

In 2014, in line with previous years, 150 women were killed by men and over 85,000 women were raped and 400,000 sexually assaulted.

As the debate reached its conclusion, it was clear that many of the young male students in black tie and penguin suits were enamoured with Buchanan.

Several young women in the debating chamber were looking uncomfortable or angry or both.

Buchanan was back on his feet, making his final comments, which focused on the illustrious university library he had visited prior to the debate. 'There are books on women in sport, women in philosophy, women in management, women in politics,' said Buchanan, 'feminist psychology, feminist theory, Black feminism, Jewish feminism, et cetera et cetera – where are the books about men?'

A female student raised her hand and said, 'Every single other book on the planet.'

> 'I am sick of men telling me that feminism is about equality.
> If I wanted to beat up my boyfriend, get turned on by his
> humiliation and spend every Friday night in a lap dance club,
> maybe that would be something to aim for.'
>
> (Sandra, young feminist group, 2020)

Often, in talking with young women about how to define feminism, the word 'equality' pops up. When I ask what they mean by the word, often they will say it means equality 'for all'. If I refine my question and ask what equality between women and men would look like, very few of them can answer.

Some will say that equality works both ways and that 'real feminists' want equality for men as well as women. But what does that even mean? Who are men wanting to be equal to? Why on earth would they want to be equal to women when we are subordinate to them?

Is feminism *really* about equality? And if so, what would a world where women and men have equal rights and status look like? If women were paid the same as men and had access to the same jobs, would it bring about an end to sexual harassment in the workplace?

To aim for equality with men as a final goal would mean that 'women's liberation' will never come to pass. If we are to strive for the rights accorded to men, that would surely deprive us of imagining a world in which women are truly liberated from male oppression.

In the early days of the women's liberation movement, feminists strove for revolution. They did not seek the opportunity to behave like men but rather to revolutionise the relationship between men and women. Feminists aimed to do away with sex stereotypes so that eventually the concept of 'gender' (by which I mean sex stereotypes and a set of imposed rules as to how women and men are supposed to behave) would be eliminated.

These early feminists were clear: men had power over women, and this had shaped personal relationships as well as every institution and every facet of social and political life. The world they sought would be dramatically different on all fronts. It would not be defined by the dynamic of domination and subordination, and all hierarchies would be challenged.

But these feminists were not popular among the general population. They were accused of being man-haters, lesbians and bitter old spinsters. Before long, the movement was taken over by 'sensible' women who focused not on men or male violence but on 'society' and legislation, such as the implementation of equality laws.

Of course, equality legislation is important because women do not have access to the same rights and privileges as men, but it stops far short of liberating women.

Equality feminism, by its very nature, is a form of liberal feminism. Feminists striving for equality, with a focus on issues such as the pay gap, has always been far more palatable for men than being told they are responsible for their own behaviour. Thorny issues like rape and domestic violence could be put to one side when they should be at the centre of such analysis, and liberal men could applaud equality feminism because it would be less threatening to their rights or power.

Under patriarchy, equality with men doesn't work out well for women. Feminists should not be seeking an equal place at the table but rather to smash the table to smithereens.

Not all things are equal

In the early 2000s, I visited a lap dance club with a difference. This one had only female customers and male dancers. I was with the former Radio Four Woman's Hour host Jenni Murray and Katherine Rake, the then-CEO of the Fawcett Society, an organisation dedicated to legal equality between women and men. Both were keen to explore women's 'sexual liberation' following decades of feminism.

We were greeted by the club manager, who said, 'Come in, girls, it's not just boys that can be naughty these days.' The club was in fact a regular strip joint for men that was turned over to female customers once a month. It was half empty, and the clientele appeared to be either hen parties or groups of young women celebrating a birthday. The male dancers looked as if they'd rather be anywhere than in a scruffy club, stripping off to R&B and spraying foam on their penises. I interviewed a few of the dancers and their stories sounded remarkably similar to those told to me by female strippers. The men had all come from typical trafficking source countries such as Hungary, Thailand and Kenya. Few could speak much English, and all had been recruited through an international agency that also recruits women into prostitution.

Each of the men told me, in one way or another, that they found the work humiliating. Ricky* said that he thought some of the female customers tried very hard to be 'as bad as men' but failed. Looking at the women's faces, with forced smiles or just sheer embarrassment, it was obvious that stepping into sexist men's shoes for the night did not exactly suit them. It seems that to enjoy the humiliation and degradation of others, you have to dehumanise them first. Not something women seem to be inclined to do; in fact women spend a lot of their time humanising men even when their behaviour least merits it. It would appear that not all things are equal.

Let's imagine a world where men are not in control. What would it look like if women's confidence was raised to a level where male approval was irrelevant? What would it feel like for women to be able to walk out after dark without fear of male violence? Do we dare to demand more than equality?

Julia Gillard is a Labour politician who served as Prime Minister of Australia between 2010 and 2013. In 2012, she made a blistering speech that had feminists all over the world punching the air with joy. Known as her 'misogyny speech', Gillard laid into the leader of the opposition for his sexism and misogyny. She opened with: 'The Leader of the Opposition says that people who hold sexist views and who are misogynists are not appropriate for high office. Well I hope the Leader of the Opposition has got a piece of paper and he is writing out his resignation. Because if he wants to know what misogyny looks like in modern Australia, he doesn't need a motion in the House of Representatives, he needs a mirror.' Julia then went on to catalogue numerous sexist remarks he had made over the years, including: 'I was offended when the Leader of the Opposition stood next to a sign that described me as a man's bitch.' Gillard was on fire, as were many other female politicians listening in the chamber. In 2020, the speech was named 'the most unforgettable moment of Australian TV history' by *Guardian Australia* readers.

But in 2019, in an opinion piece for the UK *Guardian*, Gillard was considerably tamer. Her column was inspired by that year's theme for International Women's Day (IWD), which was expressed in the hashtag #EachForEqual and described on the IWD website as 'a global day celebrating the social, economic, cultural and political achievements of women – while also marking a call to action for accelerating gender equality'. 'Gender equality is not a "women's issue",' she said. 'As the theme for IWD this year encapsulates, it is better for balance, better for all of us. Despite attempts in some quarters to paint gender equality as a zero-sum game, there are plenty of win-win propositions for these men to advocate.'

Let's unpick this argument. Had she said that violence against women is a men's issue, that would have made sense. Men are responsible for male violence towards women and therefore it should be their problem, and not left for women to deal with. But how can 'gender equality' be as much for men as for women when men as a sex class already have more power and privilege than women and can use it to exert authority and make demands over them?

The right to exclude men

Feminists have long argued that organising autonomously from men is necessary in order to be able to speak about difficult issues, such as male violence and abuse. It is also crucial in order to keep women safe. However, the ability to do this was disrupted by the 1975 Sex Discrimination Act. This created challenges for women who sought to conduct public events separately from men and proved extremely helpful to any man who hated the idea of women's autonomy

But why do so many men fear this? To state it bluntly: under patriarchy, which is based on the centrality of male dominance, women-only spaces that are informed by feminism are always seen as a threat. Women-only spaces that fit in with patriarchy, such as a college sorority, a hen night, women's charity events to raise money for safe causes, or, for that matter a brothel, are all OK.

Men can take advantage of laws that protect 'equality' in the way in which they were intended: to prioritise men's feelings over women's reality. Therefore, our oppression and the feminist response to it becomes men's opportunity to claim discrimination.

If feminism is merely about equality, then of course it would represent men as well as women. After all, what if women find that they have the same rights as men and men are forced to concede some of their institutionalised power? Might they then complain that women are 'more equal'? Would they claim that women have 'too much equality'? Have women *really* fought and died to be equal to men under patriarchy, a system which is inherently hierarchical and oppressive?

Equal opportunity to exploit?

Nothing has taught me more about the pointless quest for equality between women and men than my 2003 investigation into female sex tourism. Sick of seeing tabloid newspaper reports and cheap TV documentaries about white, primarily working-class women travelling to countries such as Jamaica and Turkey to meet young men for sex and romance in which the women were portrayed as either *really* stupid or absolutely vile, I figured that the situation might be a little more complex. I was also interested in speaking with the men involved to see how they viewed the experience.

I decided to travel to one of the infamous female tourism hotspots: the Jamaican resort of Negril, which many women visit looking for 'beach boys'. I met a number of these women and found the majority to be racist, insensitive and exploitative, to varying degrees. Most understood that the young men they were approached by in the bars were dating them in return for food and accommodation during their stay. It is a form of prostitution, and harmful for the men involved.

'Men do it all the time, why can't we?' said one sex tourist I met on the beach. 'We have the money, they really need it, and we get a bloody good shagging in return.'

Yes, deeply problematic, but no, not the same as the dynamic between older white men travelling to Cambodia or the Philippines to pay to abuse children and young women.

The system of patriarchy afforded these women some relative power. The women racially and economically exploited the men, but the men were not scared of being beaten, raped or killed, unlike their female counterparts in the sex trade.

The sex trade is, of course, one of many ways in which men continue to exploit women as a sex class, which is why feminism continues to be so necessary. But for feminism to be effective it cannot be egalitarian – it must be revolutionary. Having said that, it is fine to pursue reform in the short term, but those decisions should be made with radical analysis and uncompromising spirit.

There is a fundamental imbalance in the world between women and men, which is why women and girls need a movement of our own. 'It's impossible for us to think that we can have and replicate the exact same lives and opportunities that men have,' says author and anti-rape campaigner Winnie Li. 'But feminism has to be about restructuring the way our society is.'

In addition to the tens of thousands of rapes committed every year in England and Wales, the charity Rape Crisis has found that there are also more than 510,000 sexual assaults annually; that one in four women live with domestic abuse and, every week, between two and three women are murdered by a violent male partner. How would equality end male violence?

The writer and political activist Beatrix Campbell agrees that legal equality could not solve the massive problem of male violence, because patriarchy feeds into cultural norms: 'Millions of women live in societies where violence or death is the penalty for answering back, loving another man, loving a woman, giving birth, going to school.'

Aiming for equality as opposed to women's liberation makes space for men to use the 'women do it too' argument when trying to prove that interpersonal violence is not a male phenomenon or 'gendered'. While feminists have long acknowledged that a small minority of women perpetrate violence against male partners, this is not a 'six of one and half a dozen of the other' scenario.

As someone who has worked on this issue for decades, I can safely say that the final, fatal act of violence from a man against a woman is never the first. These women have suffered at the hands of their abusers for some time before ending up dead. As the criminologist Jane Monckton Smith discovered when examining 372 cases of women killed by a male current or ex-partner, these homicides more often than not follow a staged pattern of behaviour involving a pre-relationship history of stalking or abuse by the perpetrator; coercive control which quickly escalates in the intensity or frequency of the partner's control tactics, such as by threatening suicide; planning, such as buying weapons or finding opportunities to get the victim alone; and homicide, where the perpetrator kills the victim and possibly hurts others such as the victim's children.

Compared to the 100+ women who die annually at the hands of violent men, an average of between twelve and fifteen women kill a male partner or former partner. These are not two sides of the same coin: the overwhelming majority of women kill as a response to violence they have endured, not because they have been beating up their husbands and then go too far.

The argument that women are as violent as men in domestic violence situations is one of the most insidious but widely believed claims of the men's rights movement. There are ways to manipulate data which lend weight to this argument, for example the sort of offences that can be categorised as domestic violence, such as 'verbal abuse' (also known as 'nagging').

Many women are arrested when police are called out to a domestic violence incident, despite being the victim of an assault. There are countless stories from women who were accused of being the perpetrator because they defended themselves and caused minor injuries to the abuser.

Domestic violence statistics during the Covid-19 pandemic in 2020 showed a 50 per cent increase in both domestic homicides and reports of domestic violence in the UK. This increase was not, as been suggested by sections of the media and, surprisingly, Dr Hans Kluge, director of the World Health Organization European region, the result of perpetrators experiencing 'increased stress' but because of women's increased vulnerability and limited options to leave during lockdown.

Women and their children were killed by vengeful men, while others were left badly beaten and frightened for their lives. Counting Dead Women, which was set up in 2012 to track cases of femicide (women killed by men), recorded more than thirty domestic violence-related killings of women and children over the initial three-week period of lockdown in March and April 2020.

I asked its founder, Karen Ingala Smith, if equality would see an end to such horrendous cases of male violence. 'No' was her immediate response, as she told me that men doing half of the housework and childcare is somewhat cancelled out by the daily dose of woman-hating porn so many men consume after unloading the dishwasher. 'You're never going to get equality if one sex is the jack-off object and the other sex is the one doing the jacking off,' she said. 'It's objectification and it cements women's status in relation to men.'

More grist to the argument that equality does not provide the answer. It is necessary but it will not pave the way to liberation. And even campaigning for equality gives men the opportunity to call for even more rights than they already have *over women.*

The difference between equality and liberation

I asked Gloria Steinem, whose 1969 article 'After Black Power, Women's Liberation', brought her to fame as a feminist pioneer, if she thought that the aim of feminism is to achieve equality or liberation. She told me: 'Equality is liberation from inequality. It's the same thing.' I disagree.

Feminists do not want to become the same as the oppressors: what we want is for our difference not to be used as a tool of our oppression. We are proud of our difference, not because we celebrate being victims but because we do not want to become like the oppressors.

Equal childcare within a heterosexual relationship is impossible, even if the father takes 50 per cent responsibility for the child. It is the woman not the man who has given birth, it is her body that is in recovery, and she is the one who breastfeeds. The expectation from wider society is on the mother and not the father to be responsible. The woman is told she shouldn't drink or smoke, while the man is not constrained. If the baby doesn't develop properly, the eyes of blame are on the mother alone. If she then chooses to stay in her bedroom watching Netflix when the health visitor arrives to check on the baby, suspicion will arise. If the father did that, it is much more likely to be accepted as normal.

These double standards don't end at the childbearing stage, either, but continue all the way through parenthood because this inequality is so entrenched. But what of non-parents? In her groundbreaking research, the Swedish feminist sociologist

Carin Holmberg studied what she called 'asymmetrical role taking' by in-depth interviews with ten child-free Swedish heterosexual couples who were seen by themselves and others as having an equal relationship.

Det kallas kärlek (*It's Called Love*) (1993) is still seen as one of the most important analyses of heterosexual relationships and inherent inequality. What Holmberg found by spending time observing the couples was that, despite the men doing equal amounts of domestic chores, patterns of traditional male/female role-playing were evident in all of the relationships.

For example, when the women expressed dissatisfaction with their male partners' behaviour, they tended to accept it as 'that's how he is', whereas the men were far more likely to insist that their female partners changed the way they behaved. One of the men said that, because he didn't like small talk, he expected his partner 'not to talk to him about things that he finds uninteresting or tiring'. And the women were far more likely to try to change their behaviour in order to adapt to their partner's needs or preference; overall, they identified more with the men's view than their own.

According to Holmberg, 'In order for the man to be the way he is, the woman has to submit.' In other words, so-called equality does not necessarily give women the confidence to exercise freedom in the way that men can and do.

Ask yourself this: if it was legal for women to walk around topless in the same way it is for men, would you do it? Would you walk around in public naked from the waist up on a hot day? Or sit topless in the park? Would you go to the shops to buy groceries topless? If not, why not?

The Free the Nipple (FTN) campaign can be filed alongside Slutwalk for stupid 'feminist' ideas. FTN was started by film-maker Lina Esco in 2012 to highlight the fact that men do not get hassled when appearing topless in public, but women are not afforded the same freedom to do so. Given this is a campaign that 'empowers' women to walk around topless in public, FTN is really yet another example of women doing stuff seen as 'equality' that only benefits men. In the USA, Free the Nipple Day is celebrated on the anniversary of when North American women won the right to vote. Interestingly, walking around topless *is* legal for women in New York City, but nobody does it. I wonder why? Could it be because men's and women's breasts/nipples are not eroticised in the same way, that men's bodies are not commodified and objectified in the same way, and women know it?

Why feminism matters for men

The great irony is that men's lives will improve in many ways if they take feminism seriously, which means taking patriarchy seriously. That assumes that the short-term material benefits of being a man have to be weighed against the long-term costs of trying to 'be a man' in patriarchy, living up to distorted masculine norms. Feminism isn't for men in the sense of righting some wrong that women do to men, but it is in men's self-interest to embrace feminism in the same sense that it is in white people's self-interest to embrace anti-racism, even if it means giving up some of those short-term material advantages to do so.

Men were much more wary of feminism until it began to centre them. For instance, to celebrate International Women's Day in March 2020, the heavily male-dominated Police Service

Northern Ireland asked staff to nominate their favourite male police officers who had supported their female colleagues during their duty. But on International Men's Day, do they remember to celebrate the women who have supported their male colleagues?

If feminism was about equality then men would not be required to do anything to be seen as pro-feminist other than accept women as their equal. Very few men today, particularly the younger generations, would ever argue against equality, although they do little to promote it.

But then announcing that they are in favour of equality for women demands very little of men. Moreover, equality legislation often directly benefits them. Men are able to use equality legislation to argue that they are discriminated against, whether by women, goods and service providers, or even the state.

Student nurse Andrew Moyhing won a landmark sex-discrimination case in 2006 against the NHS hospitals that refused to let him perform intimate medical procedures on women patients unless he was accompanied by a female chaperone. The Equal Opportunities Commission said the ruling challenged assumptions that all men are sexual predators and therefore it would help to open up nursing for men, who at the time made up only 10 per cent of the workforce.

During training the previous year, Moyhing had not been allowed to provide cervical smears or electrocardiogram tests that might expose a patient's breasts unless accompanied by a female colleague. 'This was offensive to me as a man,' Moyhing told the tribunal. 'It made me feel inferior.' He said he subsequently gave up nursing because he was not allowed to 'do the job properly' in a 'female-dominated profession'.

There are many similar cases of men pleading sexual discrimination that end up in the courts. They attract the headlines because of the apparent novelty of men being the ones discriminated against in a media that frequently paints women as constant complainers.

In 2018, Thomas Bower successfully sued the pub chain BrewDog for sex discrimination after he was refused a drink that was on offer to women at a discounted rate of £4 (down from £5). BrewDog said it created Pink IPA as a way of 'exposing the sexist marketing techniques used to target women, particularly within the beer industry' and launched it as an attempt to highlight the pay gap between men and women. It also allowed 'people who identified as female' to buy the drink at a lower price than men.

Bower said that the bartender refused to sell him the drink at the discounted price on the grounds that he was male and offered him the Pink IPA for £5. Bower claimed he therefore 'felt forced to identify as female and was then able to get the drink for £4'. He later launched a claim for damages and demanded an apology for 'direct discrimination and breach of the Equality Act 2010'.

What is the point of equality legislation when it comes to men and women, if men can simply define as women? Also, how can equality legislation combat sexism when it applies equally to men? How come Bower felt no shame in ordering a drink that was dubbed, supposedly satirically, 'Beer for Girls'. The fact that he was able to identify as a woman in order to get the discounted beer shows how meaningless any talk of sexism is when sex can just be defined and adopted at will, and 'pink' is used as a symbol of womanhood.

When equality legislation directly benefits men

Feminists have been lobbying against the pinkifcation culture and the crass sexism of society since time immemorial. And, of course, many of the issues we campaign against are much more serious than simply marketing a pink beer for women.

One of the key successes of the women's liberation movement was the establishment of rape crisis centres and domestic violence refuges in the early 1970s. Not only did the feminists behind these initiatives create a sea change in public education and social attitudes regarding rape and domestic abuse, they also recognised that survivors of male violence and abuse are experts and can provide invaluable peer support to other women going through similar experiences.

The expertise of these women came from having been raised as girls under patriarchal and male supremacy, and having experienced domestic and sexual abuse. Violence perpetrated by known men, whether boyfriends, partners or ex-partners, was reframed by these survivors as one of the strategies used to control and dominate women.

In 2019, David Madden became the first male CEO of a women-only rape crisis centre in Europe. Taking up the role in Sligo, a town in the Republic of Ireland, Madden told a local journalist, 'That's the thing about gender bias, people are afraid to question it.' He meant 'gender bias' towards *men*.

Madden, who previously managed a women's drug treatment and rehabilitation centre for eight years, agreed to talk to me about what I called 'the inherent contradiction' of a man leading a women-only service. He said: 'I saw the job advertised and thought, My skills and abilities and my experience and my knowledge and qualifications – they are all a natural for this type of role.'

I asked if he thought it was fair to employ a man in such a role. 'Describing the employment of a man in a traditional female role as a slippery slope is a bit loaded,' he told me. 'I've never been challenged on that.' In one fell swoop, Madden reduced the role of running a rape crisis centre to a 'traditional female role', as though he were talking about childcare or secretarial work, and at the same time makes it clear that he feels entitled to the job because no one had challenged him.

I asked whether he had ever considered that the job should have gone to a woman, considering it is a women-only service provider? After all, there are not that many female CEOs in Ireland. 'It should be based on somebody's ability to do the job not their gender,' he said. 'I think I understand the issues a lot better than a lot of people.'

I told him it seemed very unfair on women to invite men to apply for such a role, bearing in mind how women began the rape crisis movement decades ago, building up expertise in working with traumatised women and often for no salary or official position. He replied: 'Setting down a limited criterion can also be a form of discrimination. The job should be open equally to men and to women.'

Men having it both ways

Some might argue that sex-specific job roles are redundant given that some women emphasise their similarity to men in order to argue that they deserve the same political rights, whereas others emphasise women's differences from men, arguing that women's distinctive concerns could not be adequately represented by an all-male electorate. This is the inherent contradiction of equality feminism.

In the spirit of 'feminism has gone too far'-type sexism, women can often be penalised far more harshly than men for domestic violence, even when there is scant evidence that a crime has taken place.

In December 2019, when the TV presenter Caroline Flack was accused of assaulting her male partner Lewis Burton and was subsequently arrested and charged, the police and Criminal Prosecution Service were proud of treating her as they would a man. But did they? Six police cars turned up at Flack's house after the alleged assault, following which the alleged victim had no injuries. Burton later said that he was a witness to an assault rather than a victim, suggesting that she had in fact harmed herself. In February 2020, Flack took her own life, which suggests she was deeply disturbed at the time of the alleged incident, and the treatment she received from the police and press only exacerbated her problems.

A different kind of example of contemporary media sexism comes from the protest singer Billy Bragg, who claims to be a progressive man who supports women's rights. But in March 2020 a row broke out on Twitter about whether or not male-bodied trans women should be allowed to access women-only spaces. In response to a number of feminists who argued no, Bragg tweeted: 'But surely the equality that women continue to fight for cannot be denied to others?'

When challenged on this statement, he went on to argue that his understanding of feminism is that women and girls should have the same rights as men and if that equality did not apply to everyone it is 'merely privilege'. He mused: 'What I don't understand is how some can argue that equality should be denied to a specific group.' I could almost see him scratching his head and screwing up his eyes in puzzlement. He didn't seem to understand why women-only spaces are even more necessary in a society where the pursuit of equality for all translates into more privilege for men. Yet only five years earlier, Bragg helpfully defined feminism in a tweet to mark International Women's Day: 'Let's remind ourselves . . . that a feminist is someone who believes in the empowerment of women and girls.' As a supporter of the trades union movement, I suspect Bragg would not talk about the empowerment of workers but rather a challenge to the owners in a capitalist system.

Many people assume that equality means we want the same rights and opportunities as men. But do we really want 'feminist porn' or the right to abuse men? For anti-porn feminist scholar Rebecca Whisnant, the idea of 'feminist porn' is appealing to self-identified progressives who want to defend the industry as a whole but who realise at some level that it is indefensible. Whisnant said: 'There is no such thing as feminist pornography if feminism requires, as of course it does, women's freedom as a sex class from subservience to men.'

No such pornography could sell as a mass-market product in a society premised on the sexualised subordination of women. It is a fool's errand and the material produced under the banner of 'feminist porn' is laughably shallow, mimicking the exploitative sex of mainstream porn with a few extra piercings and different gender identity combinations. We need to challenge the sham that is 'feminist porn' at every turn and recognise that the enterprise is rotten to its core.

The same argument can apply to what is termed the 'sex positivity' movement. We have already seen that harmful sexual practices such as anal gang-banging and choking are reframed under the 'choice' banner as erotic and empowering. If that sounds extreme, consider that more than a third of UK women under the age of forty have experienced unwanted slapping, choking, gagging or spitting during consensual sex, while a survey in the USA found that a quarter of women reported feeling fear during sex because their male partner unexpectedly choked them.

Non-fatal strangulation and asphyxiation are common features of domestic abuse and well-known risk indicators of homicide. Strangulation and asphyxiation are the second most common methods of murder in female homicides, and yet non-fatal strangulation is frequently used as a tool to exert power and control and to instil fear. It sends the message that 'if you do not comply, this is how easily I can kill you'.

Strangulation is extremely painful and very frightening. Loss of consciousness can occur in ten to fifteen seconds and lack of oxygen to the brain can result in mild brain damage as well as fractured trachea/larynx, internal bleeding, dizziness, nausea, tinnitus, ear bleeding, sore throat, facial and eyelid droop, loss of memory and even stroke several months later as a result of blood clots.

The Complete Manual of Breathplay (2018), written by a man named Dunter, gives an A-Z guide on all aspects of choking during sex. Dunter warns of the dangers, revealing that he has lost 'many friends' through 'breath play gone wrong', but explains how 'from physical sensation to simple mind games, people are doing it to fulfil different needs'.

And there is plenty of advice on how to be safe during BDSM and kink-fuelled sex, including in *Cosmopolitan* magazine, which you can pick up while you are in the supermarket shopping for bread and milk. If the choice brigade excuses the worst violence that happens to women, how do they expect anything else to be challenged?

Chapter 4

An Ism of One's Own:
Putting the Politics Back into Identity

'I am not free while any woman is unfree even when
her shackles are very different from my own.'

Audre Lorde

'Listen to Sex Workers!' (No, not *that* one)

In April 2016 I headed to Melbourne to attend the very
first conference on prostitution in Australia organised by
feminists against the sex trade. Victoria is a state with one of
the world's oldest legalised systems of brothel prostitution. I
wanted to meet the women who had survived this system.

The sex trade is reliant on misogyny, poverty and class
prejudice, racism, colonialism and imperialism. Anyone needing a straightforward lesson in what intersectionality means in
practice need look no further than the sex trade. Poor, black,
brown and indigenous women do the heavy lifting in prostitution, and the lower status in the eyes of the buyers the women
are, the worse they are treated.

When I arrived at the conference venue, Melbourne University campus, a group of protesters had set up camp outside the
entrance and were holding placards and shouting through

loudhailers: 'sex work is work', 'blow jobs are real jobs', and 'trans-women are women'. Not only were the protesters angry about feminists criticising the sex trade, labelling us SWERFs (sex worker exclusionary radical feminists), they also dubbed us TERFs (transgender exclusionary radical feminists) because, as one protester shouted, 'Trans women sex workers of colour are dying thanks to SWERFs!'

'Intersectional feminism lives here!' shouted the crowd, waving placards towards the delegates and speakers entering the venue.

Every event I attended during my trip (including this conference) was prefaced with some statement of this kind:

We acknowledge that we are on the lands of the Wurundjeri people who have been custodians of this land for thousands of years and acknowledge and pay our respects to their Elders past and present.

In the conference, there were many indigenous and other women of colour, both as speakers and delegates. 'White men would target us as children because they knew the police wouldn't care,' Caro says. 'Native girls are worth even less than white girls in their eyes, and as far as the johns were concerned, we were bred for prostitution.'

Speaker after speaker spoke of intersecting oppressions experienced by so many prostituted women. But every survivor I met at the conference told me that the supporters of the sex trade, such as those shouting 'SWERF' and 'TERF' outside, ignore the issues of race, indigenous status, class and misogyny when it comes to prostitution.

'They call me a racist – a "white feminist",' says Sammie, an indigenous woman and sex-trade survivor. 'I suppose defending white, rich pimps and johns, and the "happy hookers" who dip in and out of high-class escorting gives them a few more pats on the back than standing up for the women at the bottom of the pile.'

The following day, in a packed room above an Italian restaurant in Melbourne, I prepared to launch *Prostitution Narratives: Stories of Survival in the Sex Trade,* a collection of twenty first-person accounts by women who had left the sex trade. The stories recounted the violence, abuse and long-lasting effects of prostitution, such as post-traumatic stress disorder (PTSD), disassociation, depression and anxiety. But the stories were also full of hope.

Many of the contributors were at the launch, looking proud and nervous in equal measure. Some of the women would be reading extracts of their own writing, and it was a big deal. Listening to their stories I could not help but feel a rising anger: teenagers snatched from care homes by pimps; girls raped by family members and running away from home and into the clutches of exploiters; and young women of colour marketed as 'exotic' to men in strip joints.

Sometime later, my anger rose several notches higher, when I heard from several of the contributors about the protests that took place at subsequent launches across Melbourne and elsewhere. A Brisbane launch had to be moved from a domestic violence service due to threats by pro-sex-trade advocates, whose members did their best to get the service defunded. At another event, one of the contributors, a woman who had been prostituted from the age of five, was harassed by a 'sex work is work' lobbyist who told her she should go back into prostitution but move to New South Wales where the 'working conditions' in the brothels are 'much better'.

I travelled back to the UK with Rachel Moran, sex-trade survivor and author of *Paid For: My Journey Through Prostitution*. 'Thank Christ those "blow jobs are real jobs" protesters weren't around when I was trying to get out of the sex trade,' she said. 'I would still be in it today.'

Feminism, at its best, has always adhered to the principle that is now known as intersectionality, and this was already fundamental to the practice of most thoughtful feminists. As famously explained by Kimberlé Crenshaw, 'intersectionality' is a useful term which shows that when multiple forms of oppressions meet, they create new oppressions that are experienced acutely by those who belong to certain marginalised groups.

How I would explain it is by using the example of prostitution. Although prostitution is a form of exploitation that overwhelmingly affects women and girls, it is specifically poor and indigenous women, and women of colour who are most at risk. A number of (white) sex buyers I have interviewed have told me that they often select specific women on the basis of racist and colonialist stereotypes. Ethnicity itself is eroticised in prostitution. One man said: 'I had a mental check list in terms of race; I have tried them all over the last five years but they turned out to be the same.' Another interviewee openly admitted that his use of Chinese women in prostitution was in order to fulfil a fantasy that he held about them. 'You can do a lot more with the Oriental girls like blow job without a condom, and you can cum in their mouths . . . I view them as dirty.'

It is impossible to understand the system of prostitution without being attentive to the influence of sex, race and economic class; without, in other words, taking an intersectional approach.

The misappropriation of intersectionality

In its intended form, intersectionality is a useful political tool that formalises the inclusion of race and difference in feminist theory, in the way that Marxism theorised class. But like so many other useful political concepts, it can be hijacked by those with their own political agenda. For the feminist writer Chimamanda Ngozi Adichie, 'the term "intersectional" can often be used by white feminists to virtue signal as well as to misinterpret and pour scorn on the feminism of white women'. When we met in London in 2019 Adichie was keen to talk about the way in which some 'woke white women' feel entitled to lecture black feminists on 'intersectional' politics. She recalls a white woman lecturing her about the true origins of Kimberlé Crenshaw's theory. '"Intersectional" has become a word thrown at women to silence them,' she says.

One group that has very successfully misappropriated the term 'intersectional' is men who hate any feminism except the 'fun' kind, where they are in charge and ordering women to bake cupcakes for an English Collective of Prostitutes fund-raiser. Because it would look bad if these men spent their time shouting at black women on the internet about feminism, they instead go after (actual) white feminists in an attempt to discredit political positions held by feminists of all races and ethnicities, such as a critique of the sex trade, surrogacy and religious fundamentalism.

A prime example of men leaping on this particular bandwagon occurred at Washington's march against Trump in

2017. Perched on a plinth a little above the crowds were two young white men, sporting full beards and smug, superior expressions, standing either side of two young black women. The men were each holding the poles of a huge banner with an emblazoned slogan, 'White feminism was built on the back of women of color'. Several puzzled marchers stopped to take photographs. Here they were, helping two black women pour scorn on 'white feminism'. Their responsibility as part of the patriarchy had been eroded and replaced with the perfect opportunity to denounce the witches whilst being seen as the good guys.

The 'white feminism' slur is often used not as a reasonable critique but as a handy slur against women that campaign against sexual exploitation. Despite the fact that so many sex-trade survivors are indigenous, of colour and black, abolitionists are often labelled 'racist' or 'colonialist' too because, according to sex-trade apologists, their actions prevent women of colour from earning a living through prostitution.

Kenneth Roth is one of a number of white, powerful and highly paid men in the human rights (aka men's rights) world who supports the abuse of poor women of colour in the sex trade by framing it as 'choice'. During the campaign by Amnesty International to adopt a policy of blanket decriminalisation of the sex trade, Roth tweeted in response to kickback from abolitionists: 'All want to end poverty, but in meantime why deny poor women the option of voluntary sex work?' Sex-trade survivor, Rachel Moran, responded with: 'Ken Roth, wouldn't you say, if a person cannot afford to feed themselves, the appropriate thing to put in their mouth is food, not your cock?'

Intersectionality has been distorted into almost the opposite of its original intended meaning. As an example, there have been a number of working-class lesbians, many whom are of colour, told that they are oppressing white natal males who identify as non-binary. This is a story I hear time and time again from young feminists who have been bullied out of expressing their views.

I am constantly approached by young female students who tell me they feel bullied into accepting that 'sex work is work' while wondering why so many leftist men are not listening to the women of colour who name prostitution as racist and colonialist. Young socialist women querying the inherent abuse of poor and marginalised working-class women are told to shut up and avoid White Feminists.

These young feminists understand that the oppression they face as women is structural and not based on individual identities. And yet they see 'progressives' not only demonise those who *actually* spend their time protesting and organising against male violence and patriarchy, but also support the status quo by glamorising and promoting the very things feminists are protesting against. The greatest irony of all is that, despite hurling around accusations of 'white feminism', these same 'progressive' voices will regularly censor and no-platform women of colour who campaign against male violence while prioritising the placement of trans women (people born as men) on those platforms instead.

This bastardised version of intersectionality has gained popularity alongside the new 'Queer' identity politics where identity is about individual definitions as opposed to structural, material oppression.

It undermines a more radical approach to tackling male power, as it promotes a neoliberal position on the veil, pornography and prostitution, surrogacy and extreme transgender ideology. Feminists that critique such ideologies and practices are accused of being practising 'white feminists' whatever our race and ethnicity. To argue that the sex trade is bad for women, surrogacy is exploitation, and women do not enjoy being strangled during sex until they pass out often earns us the labels of 'prude' and 'regressive'.

The rise of the trans movement has further undermined the sex-class analysis on which feminism depends. Feminism is rooted in the understanding that sex is about innate biological characteristics that determine whether or not we are male or female, and gender is a social construction based on sex stereotypes.

Trans activists insist on denying the importance of biological sex to women's experiences, and some feminists have folded to their demands, believing themselves to be showing compassion to a marginalised and vulnerable group. In practice, this means that a distorted interpretation of an intersectional feminist approach often prioritises the interests of men over those of women and results in a chaotic system in which any bad-faith actor can lay claim to be a member of an oppressed minority.

Perhaps one of the more glaring failures of the neo-intersectionalists is the failure to recognise class, and how class prejudice affects women in particular.

When, in 2017, I was invited to speak at the Salford Working Class Movement Library on my experiences of growing up as a working-class lesbian in the north-east of England, such was the vitriol from the LBGTQQIA+ activists – none of whom had ever made use of the library's amazing resources – that the volunteers were almost forced to cancel the sell-out event. When the steering committee refused to back down, the protesters targeted the library funders in an attempt to persuade them to drop support for the resource. There was no solidarity with the unpaid volunteers that keep the only such library running on a shoestring. I was not intending to speak about anything relating to transgender issues, but that did not seem to matter.

Outside the venue was a small group of protesters, all from the University of Manchester. Several were shouting slogans relating to being non-binary, and, from what I could gather from their accents and sense of entitlement, all appeared to be from middle- to upper-middle-class backgrounds. The very idea that a non-binary identity could trump that of a working-class girl coming out as a lesbian on a council estate was quite astounding.

TERF wars

Vaishnavi Sundar, a filmmaker from South India and the founder of Women Making Films, has worked with marginalised women all her life and campaigns against male violence. Sundar successfully fought for women to be able to access morning-after contraception in the state of Tamil Nadu, and has all-round impeccable feminist credentials.

Recognising the enormity of the problem of sexual harassment of women in the Indian workplace, her second big project involved crowdfunding in 2018 to make a film on the topic as a way to hold the Indian criminal justice system to account for the lack of implementation of its law against sexual harassment.

The project was an arduous one but Sundar was determined to get the voices of lower-caste women heard. 'I shot for more than a year all over India,' she says. 'I made sure I captured every possible known demographic of the working woman.' The film, *But What Was She Wearing?*, was finished in 2020 and Vaishnavi secured screenings in North America before showing it in India. Her reputation is such that Sundar and her work are always warmly welcomed in both the Global North and South. But shortly before a screening of the film in New York, she was emailed by the organisers and told that she was no longer welcome and the event was cancelled along with Sundar and her film.

'I was told I was transphobic and they cited tweets as evidence, such as "A safe space for trans women is not inside a woman's bathroom",' she explains. 'Transgenderism had nothing to do with the film. It was about sexual abuse of low-status women.'

The email informing Sundar that she was cancelled did not invite a right to reply or any kind of defence; it was a fait accompli. 'This is a huge blow for my future films,' she says. 'I rely a lot on crowdfunding. I believe in making a film as a community. Now, ninety per cent of those that support my films will no longer support me because I am labelled as a bigot.'

Despite being effectively no-platformed across the whole of New York, Sundar's film has resulted in a number of Indian women taking their employers to tribunals, and many women in low-paid jobs have created informal unions to support each other in dealing with sexual harassment. *But What Was She Wearing?* has inspired women to pursue the case against their harassers to positive effect.

'Until my film, not a lot of people were even aware of the legal obligation of a workplace to deal with sexual harassment cases, especially smaller companies, and some companies even invite me in to talk to them about sexual harassment in India,' she says. Yet this is the sort of activism that the New York organisation, which considers itself extremely progressive, wants to shut down because of Sundar's unrelated views on trans issues which it deemed to be bigoted.

A similar thing happened to Raquel Rosario Sanchez, who came to the UK from the Dominican Republic in 2017. Rosario Sanchez had been accepted on a scholarship to complete a PhD about sex buyers at the Centre for Gender and Violence Research at the University of Bristol.

In February 2018, she was invited to chair a meeting for A Woman's Place UK, about women's sex-based rights. As soon as the event was advertised, the targeting by trans activists began and focused almost exclusively on Rosario Sanchez and not the (white, British) panellists. The campaign against her and the event was vicious and well coordinated, involving hundreds of students and many others, even though the talk was off-campus and in no way affiliated to the university. There were demands that the meeting be cancelled amid claims that harm would somehow be caused to trans people if it went ahead.

'The university's immediate response was to question me,' she says. 'I had emails from the media office and from campus security who saw the vilification and decided the guilty party must have been me.' On the night of the meeting, a number of masked trans activists asking about the whereabouts of the venue posted photographs of themselves on social media and were, in Rosario Sanchez's words, 'like predators searching for prey'.

After failing to persuade their university to cancel the meeting, the Intersectional Feminist Society presented a motion at the Bristol Student Union Annual General Meeting in late February 2018, which sought to 'ban all TERFs from speaking on campus'. The motion was voted favourably by students, and the few young women who spoke out against it were shouted down. But the attempt at no-platforming trans-critical feminists was not passed by the university and Rosario Sanchez and other women labelled 'TERFs' regularly speak there, and set up the Women Talk Back! monthly consciousness-raising groups, affiliated to the student union, as a consequence. In 2020, I spoke at a packed event they organised on the global sex trade.

Rosario Sanchez filed a complaint against the transgender student who began the campaign but, each time a disciplinary hearing opened, balaclava-clad trans activists would protest outside. This resulted in three separate hearings being shut down. At the attempted hearings, trans activists distributed a pamphlet entitled 'Why We Fight the TERF War', in which students were encouraged to yell 'Scum! Scum! Scum!' and 'You're shit and you know you are' at women attending to support her.

'For a young Dominican woman like me, coming to study in the United Kingdom felt like a dream come true,' she says. 'But these past two years have been an absolute nightmare. I was publicly bullied and harassed by throngs of privileged British students who were making a sport out of targeting an immigrant.'

Trans politics is giving a generation of privileged, mostly white, people from the Global North a weapon with which to continue to exploit the marginalised by appropriating an analysis that is meant to challenge and overthrow structural inequality.

'I come from a country in the Global South where child marriage is predominant and teen pregnancy is an active barrier to the education of a large percentage of our girls. Watching these wealthy, white students at the University of Bristol play pretend at Oppression Olympics, making a game out of abusing me, made me sick.'

De-platforming feminists

I have also been regularly silenced and de-platformed. Note that I don't say 'no-platformed', which is an important distinction because de-platforming refers to women who have been invited to speak but that invitation is then revoked following complaints from so-called progressives. No-platforming is when organisations have a list of individuals that will never be offered a speaking slot because their views would be likely to incite violence and genuine harm, or at least that is how it used to work.

This de-platforming began in 2008 when the National Union of Students added me to a list of fascist and racist groups – and former dictators – as a person that they would not share a platform with. Individuals at elite institutions established what would become policy across many student bodies of bullying women who spoke out against extreme transgender ideology, and denying them a platform from which to speak about feminism.

Since January 2004, when I wrote an article headlined 'Gender Benders, Beware' in the *Guardian Weekend* magazine, whenever it becomes public that I am about to speak at an event, always about an aspect of male violence and always as part of my campaigning work as opposed to paid journalism, a mob forms with the aim of bullying the organisers into un-inviting me. This is always played out in public and is always humiliating. Usually, the organisers capitulate.

Whenever I or other feminists that are targeted by Queer ISIS are cancelled from an event publicly complain, we are asked why we 'assume' the right to a public platform. I don't. What I reasonably assume is that once I have accepted an invitation to speak, and the event has been widely advertised, tickets sold, trains and accommodation booked and, on many occasions, my talk prepared, the organisers do not cave to pressure and denounce me in order to appease the bullies.

What I find upsetting is when students approach me by email or public events and ask if I would come and speak to their university about sexual violence, for example. They want to hear what I have to say but are denied the opportunity.

At the fiftieth-anniversary Women's Liberation Movement conference, academic historian Selina Todd, who has written about working-class women's lives that would otherwise be forgotten, was de-platformed for having the tenacity to speak out against the disappearance of women under the extreme transgender doctrine that is becoming commonplace across academic institutions.

The writer and activist Lola Olufemi was also due to speak at the conference, not alongside Todd but on a separate panel. She decided to use the opportunity to cancel herself from the event and have a statement read out on her behalf by another of the young intersectional feminists: 'I have seen first-hand how white middle-class women with social capital have used their gatekeeping power to harass trans-people, threaten them with deformation, actively work to curtail their rights, refuse to extend solidarity and then claim victimhood.'

Olufemi is suggesting that only white middle-class women with institutional privilege are opposed to extreme transgender ideology. She is wrong.

Firstly, because many black and working-class liberation feminists recognise that they have the most to lose if we lose our sex-based rights. Women of colour, including and as well as women who are poor and on low income, rely on services and facilities that protect them from male violence. These women are also far more likely to be in prison, psychiatric wards, care homes and detention centres than their white, privileged counterparts. And secondly, because the majority of white feminists who are campaigning for women's sex-based rights are not in any way hostile to trans people and have repeatedly argued for their rights to dignity and safety.

White Feminism?

All the same, the theory that middle-class, white, 'privileged' women are the problem does not go away. In her charmingly titled Vice article 'Ban Sex Work? Fuck Off, White Feminism', trans activist Paris Lees states that 'White Feminism is a special club but membership doesn't rest solely on race. White Feminism is about privilege.'

By this logic, black women can be white feminists. It takes some gall for a white person raised as a boy to decide who is white and who can properly define themselves as feminist.

Lees further describes these 'white feminists' as 'Ladies who lunch and feel hard done by because a man held the door open for them on their way in to the Four Seasons.'

What have these women done to provoke Lees into labelling them as such? Well, they campaigned to end prostitution, and

113

just as the feminist academics saw their work derailed by the progressives, now the media-savvy trans lobby is further derailing genuine feminist activism.

Further 'crimes' include being ready to support those women who wish to leave the sex trade and putting the blame for the problems of prostitution on the punters rather than the women.

For Lees, if one is trans it is impossible to also be a 'white feminist': 'I am both white and a feminist. But I am not what you would call a White Feminist, capital letters, for I am also trans.' So Caitlyn Jenner, a very rich, powerful white trans woman with a huge media profile and social capital could likewise never be labelled as such. Even though Jenner is a former Trump supporter. And neither could Kellie Maloney, formerly a boxing promoter called Frank who once admitted on live television that he would procure prostituted women for his male friends in the boxing world to abuse, and who is a former member of UKIP.

There we have it: the point clearly spelled out to us by natal men. Former pimps and racists who were men but now identify as women are exempt from the accusation of being white feminists, while those of us who fight to end male violence on behalf of all women are fair game for being tarred with the 'white feminist' brush.

Blue fringes and unicorns

In the late 1980s, identity politics dominated feminist activism. I called it having an 'ism of one's own', because most meetings would begin with individuals laying claim to their credentials, such as 'speaking as a lesbian mother/of Asian descent/working-class'. It became ridiculous when micro-identities began to dominate. Of course, some women had multiple oppressions but sometimes most of the meeting would be taken up with statements such as: 'Speaking as a Jewish, working-class, fat, lesbian . . .'

Working-class women and women of colour were abundant in the movement. However, despite engaging with feminists who should know better, the working-class women and women of colour continually needed to ask others to consider whether their speech or actions were racist or classist. Similarly, disabled women would take event organisers to task for not considering whether venues were accessible, and mothers of small children would rightly be annoyed if a conference failed to organise a crèche.

Consequently, the issues of race, class and disability divisions in the movement became irreparable. For example, Jewish lesbians were split along lines such as their differing views about the conflict in the Middle East, as well as lesbianism, class and their Ashkenazi or Sephardic origins. Women of colour might be divided about any combination of other issues such as class, sexuality or disability and disabled women could be conflicted regarding race, ethnicity or motherhood. These are just a few examples.

The identity politics of the 1980s did, in part, come about for good reason, which was that the women's movement was challenging the silencing of voices from history, and the most silenced voices then started to demand to be heard, including those of black women and lesbians. Which is all good until you find yourself needing to be oppressed (aside from being female) in order to be allowed a voice at all.

Socialist men have grown fond of using identity politics against feminists. For example, some men find it impossible not to point out that working-class women and women of colour suffer multiple oppressions without suggesting or blatantly stating that white middle-class women have lives of privilege and luxury. These same men will use 'intersectional' arguments against those of us fighting male violence in a way that is clearly motivated by misogyny as opposed to genuine concern about marginalised women. Many of the same men on Twitter who hail intersectionality also hurl abuse such as 'TERF' and 'bigot' at those of us who criticise the sex trade and extreme transgender ideology.

Those who consider the singer Sam Smith to be oppressed because, on occasion, people forget to use their chosen pronouns, might find it difficult to appreciate why women campaigning to end rape and domestic homicide don't empathise.

When it comes to identities such as being polyamorous or the ubiquitous and all-encompassing 'queer', there is often no identity whatsoever. However, people of colour, women, lesbians and gay men all suffer structural oppression and their identities are rooted in material reality, and tend not to be picked up and put down on a whim.

There is no shortage of white middle-class trans women who claim to be oppressed by women. Many of them also criticise feminists for racism. The argument goes like this: 'excluding trans women from the category of woman is the same as excluding black women from the category of woman', which then extends to 'excluding black women from the category of human'. So, by not accepting that trans women are *actual* women we are saying that we don't accept that black women are women *or* human. This is an extraordinary twist of logic.

Trans-plaining is commonplace in discussions about sexism where any and every topic is hijacked so that it becomes about trans issues. Take an episode of the podcast 'The Ciscourse' that was broadcast on 14 May 2018, featuring the Momentum activist and Novara Media journalist Ash Sarkar in conversation with the trans activist and journalist Shon Faye. Faye, who is white, was sympathising with Sarkar, who is Asian, about the times she had been spoken over and had her concerns dismissed by white women, saying: 'As white women, we can tend to be, like, "Mm, but what about the sexism we experience?"'

For starters, despite being raised as a man, Faye claims to have experienced far more sexism than Sarkar ever has. Faye then went on to trans-plain further by explaining how a 'cisgender woman' might respond to complaints about transphobia 'with something about the fact that she has given birth, or the gendered labour she has had to perform throughout her life, or whatever, and that's true but it's not about transphobia'.

To me, Faye made it clear that the needs and rights of trans women should always trump those of natal women and the 'sexism' referred to was seemingly second to the experiences of trans women. In fact, women complaining about our oppression is, as far as Faye is concerned, transphobic because it marginalises the experiences of trans women.

'You can say whatever misogynistic thing you like,' says Naomi Bridges, a young feminist campaigner from London, 'but if you put "white feminist" or "TERF" at the end of it you can feel righteous because they're the enemy. These terms being weaponised against feminists is such a godsend to men.'

The writing out of black and working-class feminists

Black women have always played a major role in the movement, a fact that is erased by the myth that it was exclusively organised by and for white middle-class women. Anti-FGM campaigner Nimco Ali is a black feminist, a survivor of FGM and a refugee from Somalia to the UK. She says she is tired of hearing white women claim that feminism is dominated by white middle-class women because it assumes that feminism only exists in the West. 'I see feminists on a global agenda,' says Ali. 'There are women across the world doing this in their own communities. That doesn't also mean that just because you're a white middle-class woman you don't also have struggles.'

Gloria Steinem points out that ever since the first Louis Harris American Women's Opinion Poll about the women's liberation movement in 1972, black women have been twice as likely as white women to support the movement and all its issues, from equal pay to reproductive justice, but this evidence is disregarded as it doesn't fit the narrative. She says: 'Of course, the media often exclude black women and other women of colour from stories about the women's movement and may also report more about black men than black women in the civil rights movement.' There is a feeling that the media's exclusion of black women implies these women were not involved in the early campaigns, when of course they were.

White, middle-class feminists did play a prominent role in the history of feminism. Many of the early books about the history of feminism were written by white, middle-class writers. The founder of the Women's Social and Political Union, Emmeline Pankhurst, was often seen as the face of the women's suffrage movement and there was a dominant section of the movement that was led by white middle-class women. However, this ignores the factory workers and other women who worked alongside her, as well as the women who had gone before Pankhurst and on whose shoulders she and other feminists have stood. Annie Kenney is the most well-known example of a working-class woman who became a leading militant suffragette, after the former mill worker from Lancashire met Christabel Pankhurst at a rally and the two became firm friends. Jill Liddington's excellent book *One Hand Tied Behind Us* (1978) depicts how the radical suffragists of Manchester and the Lancashire cotton towns took their message out to women at the grassroots, to the Co-operative Guilds and trade union branches, and offers innumerable examples of strong, working-class women who took up the campaign.

Ella Whelan is the assistant editor at the online political magazine *Spiked*. She says she despises feminism because, she claims, it is riddled with women who hate working-class people. 'I don't call myself a feminist because it would make my skin crawl to position myself with the middle-class professional feminists,' she says. 'I have a huge, massive chip on my shoulder about the way that they treat working-class women and how they talk about people like my family. I really despise them.'

I have no idea what brought Whelan to her views on feminism. Perhaps she has not spent enough time with the women fighting for rights of women from the bottom of the pile, and has encountered the 'lean-in' types that go on about glass ceilings? Either way, it would be impossible for her not to have noticed that the loudest, most successful feminist campaigns are those that challenge violence against women in the home, and that the women with no or little means of escape or justice are poor and otherwise disenfranchised women.

Feminism is for all women and continues to have a purpose until we are no longer the victims of male violence by virtue of being women. Yet today, we are told that it is bigotry and that hatred towards women and our bodies is progressive and feminist. It is more important than ever that we re-establish the principles of liberation feminism while moving forward without the backlash that has dogged our movement in recent years, and encourage a new generation of proud, critical and vocal feminists to step forward.

Chapter 5

A Woman's Right to Choose?
A Smokescreen for Men's Abuse

'People who have power do not daydream about empowerment.'

(Marcie Bianco, 2017)

'You didn't make good choices. You HAD good choices.'

(Mia to Elena, *Little Fires Everywhere*)

What happens in Vegas . . .

Vienna is not my favourite city. The food is awful, unless you eat nothing but cake and wurst, and everyone seems to smoke and to speak only German.

Nevertheless, off to Vienna I went in April 2015 to attend an international conference on 'sex work'.

The sex trade in Austria's capital city is booming. Prostitution is legal and it is not unusual to see vehicles carrying adverts for brothels and strip clubs driving around Westbahnhof station, an area which connects the central red-light districts. Such a blatant display of merchandising female flesh would not have troubled the vast majority of conference delegates – only four out of the 185 attendees considered prostitution to be a human rights violation. The conference consensus was that 'sex work is work' and blanket decriminalisation of all aspects of prostitution would solve its inherent problems.

A few academics from the University of Nevada in Las Vegas (UNLV), such as sociology professor Barb Brents, gave presentations. Brents supports legalisation on the grounds that it can reduce stigmatisation and that legalised prostitution can be 'empowering' for certain women. Delegates were treated to photographs of the inside of a Nevada brothel.

Christina Parreira, a doctoral candidate at UNLV, was studying prostitution in the state's legal brothels and, as part of her research, sold sex in a Nevada brothel for 36 days. She wrote on the Bunny Ranch blog. 'Sex work is definitely not my last resort or my only option – it is my choice. I'd like to continue to have the opportunity to make that choice legally.'

Parreira spoke at the conference about her doctoral research on sexual desire at 'work' telling the audience that 'older sex workers' found it easier to orgasm with 'clients' than younger women.

The brothel in which Parreira conducted her research was owned by Dennis Hof, Nevada's best-known legal pimp, who, at the time of his death in 2018, was being investigated for various sexual crimes against women, including rape and trafficking.

Sitting in the conference and listening to the Nevada system being hailed in glowing terms took me right back to my research trip to several of Hof's legal brothels in 2011.

It was midday when I arrived at the Moonlite Bunny Ranch in rural Nevada. Within minutes I witnessed the line-up. When a punter rang the doorbell, any 'unoccupied' women had one minute to appear in the reception area and were required to stand with a smile on their faces until the punter made his choice.

I was given permission by Hof to speak to a number of the 'girls' on the premises. One was Lynn, who invited me into the room in which she both lives and provides sexual 'services'.

Lynn's bedroom, painted hot pink and with a mirrored ceiling, had pornographic photographs of her on the wall. A small video screen perched on the mantelpiece showed footage of Lynn having sex with punters. The dressing table was bare except for lubricant, condoms, tissues and sex toys.

Lynn told me that it was 'fun' at the brothel. 'Some people say that we are locked in when we are here,' said Lynn, 'but Daddy [Hof] isn't like that. We can go out whenever we wish.'

Perched on the edge of the bed, Lynn was dressed for 'work' in hotpants and a bikini top and appeared to be choosing her words very carefully. When she told me how much she enjoyed seeing 'clients', and that they were all clean, decent, and mostly good-looking, I didn't question her, although my impression of the punters I had seen at the bar did not quite fit that description. 'I love what I do, and it is my choice,' Lynn told me. 'I know feminists don't like hearing that, but maybe I just love sex.'

We finished the interview and, as I was leaving, I made a comment about how tidy and sparse her room was.

'Do you not have any of your personal things here?' I asked her, thinking how miserable it must be to both live and work in one room and not even have reminders of home for comfort.

Opening her bedside drawer, Lynn took out a framed photograph of a beautiful little girl, aged about six or seven, and, smiling, held it up so I could see. 'This is my daughter,' she said. 'But I keep it hidden away from those men, because I don't want those bastards looking at her, or their horrible spermy hands touching my little girl.'

'My body, my choice' is one of the most recognised slogans of second-wave feminism. This is because, prior to the many achievements of the women's liberation movement, women's lives were defined by the *absence* of choice.

Women who choose to be anti-feminists do so because they have vested interests, whether it's because of their career, their marriage, or generally seeking approval from men. They worry that by taking a more principled feminist stand their life will be that bit more difficult for them and men might not find them quite so attractive and delightful.

We need to find new strategies for combating anti-feminism because it keeps metamorphosing into a different form. To view prostitution as a choice ignores the reality, and men often use women's choices as a smokescreen to justify their own behaviour. They say things like 'women want to be choked; women like pornography; women want to sell sex; women want to wear the veil'.

Women had little or no choice concerning whether they married or had children, or even about sexual practice and pleasure. Feminism created a landscape in which women could, to an extent, exercise choice. However, as the legal impediments to women's participation in the public sphere began to disappear in the 1970s, 'choice' took on a different meaning and started to become about individual choice and agency. For instance, until the 1970s, if a woman chose to buy a washing machine on hire purchase, she needed a man such as her husband or father to sign the paperwork; she wasn't able to take out the loan agreement on her own. It is important to distinguish this 'choice' from the language of 'choice', which has become a consumerist concept as opposed to a real choice about women determining what happens to our bodies and ourselves.

These days, it is apparently 'choice feminism' to say that any decision made by a woman – whether that is a decision to have a cheese sandwich for lunch or to take her clothes off and strip for men for money – is a feminist one, simply because it is a woman making that decision. This is not real feminism.

Feminism should pose a serious challenge to patriarchy, and if it doesn't then it is not real feminism. Liberal and postmodern feminism softens that challenge by talking less about patriarchy and the actual material realities of women's lives and more about women's 'choice' and 'agency'. That continues to be particularly true on issues such as prostitution, pornography and surrogacy.

'Our collective commitment to human dignity demands that we not turn away from the reality of the world in which we all make decisions,' says Robert Jensen, author of *The End of Patriarchy: Radical Feminism for Men* (2017), 'including those harsh realities that affect people without wealth, power, privilege, and status.'

The rise of 'choice feminism'

What we now recognise as 'choice feminism' began in the 1990s with the Spice Girls' vapid slogan of 'girl power'. This phenomenon emerged at the same time as sexist 'lads' mags' such as *Zoo* and *Loaded*. A sample 1995 issue of *Loaded* featured a guide to the best kebab shops next to 'The Wonderful World of Trolley Dollies', which was a feature of 'confessions' of female cabin crew. A competition run by *Zoo* to 'win a boob job for your girlfriend' attracted more than 200 entries.

Choice feminism really just panders to men who like nothing better than women saying that they 'choose' prostitution, stripping, having children, getting married, taking their husband's name and acting as surrogates. And why do men like this? Because it suits them to keep women in subordinate positions where they can continue to exploit them.

Men also jumped on the bandwagon when they began using 'choice' to justify and excuse behaviour such as going to strip clubs, paying for sex and going out to work while their wives stayed at home to raise the children. In the eyes of men, this was all about being progressive. This is beautifully summed up in the 2011 romcom *Crazy, Stupid, Love* when Ryan Gosling's character says, 'The war between the sexes is over. We won the second women started pole dancing for exercise.' How miserably true that is, and was aped perfectly in a piece on *The Onion* satirical website: 'Whereas early feminists campaigned tirelessly for improved health care and safe, legal access to abortion, often against a backdrop of public indifference or hostility, today's feminist asserts control over her biological destiny by wearing a baby-doll T-shirt with the word "Hoochie" spelled in glitter.'

The argument within feminism about choice is not new. In the early second wave, feminists were criticised for attacking women who wanted to wear make-up, get married, or who chose to stay home and raise a family. But feminists were not and are not attacking other women for what they choose. Rather we are asking, 'What are the forces that shape choices?' and in doing so, we are considering what the rewards and punishments are for the 'choices' women make, and naming the potential impacts on girls and young women when they see women embracing 'choices' that effectively disempower them.

Fiona McKenzie, founder of the feminist campaign group We Can't Consent to This, says that when she first became a feminist in 2016, in her mid thirties, things were 'pretty bad for women', but she has noticed how much worse things have become in the past four years, in particular for young women. 'We're all enraged by the nonsense young women face, such as choking in sex being normal and fun.'

#She&HeforHe

One of the aims of feminism is to expose a false ideology that contributes to the oppression of women. And the underlying ideology regarding concepts of choice is liberalism, something the actor Emma Watson has made popular via her #HeForShe initiative. Watson, who is best known for her role in the *Harry Potter* film series, created the hashtag to implore men to support women in our quest for liberation. However, #HeForShe fell as flat as my lockdown sourdough and made about as much difference to women's welfare as David Cameron wearing a 'This is What a Feminist Looks Like' T-shirt.

#HeForShe has the key aim to get men to pledge to 'take action against all forms of violence and discrimination faced by women and girls'. And yet in the six years since it was launched, there has been an increase rather than a reduction in the incidence of male violence towards women and girls. According to the World Health Organization (WHO) in the years 2015–2019 femicide, rape and sexual assault, and forced marriage are more prevalent than in the decade prior to the data collection.

127

Emma Watson seems to believe that feminism is about 'choice'. That's right, the privileged young woman who sailed through life being able to choose a top-notch education and drama school has come up with a brilliant idea for women's emancipation. And that idea is that we choose our way out of our oppression. As she explained to *Elle* magazine in 2014: 'If you want to run for prime minister, you can. If you don't, that's wonderful, too. Shave your armpits, don't shave them, wear flats one day, heels the next. We want to empower women to do exactly what they want.' She has been rightly ridiculed by all and sundry for promoting 'superficial feminism' that is utterly meaningless and useless to any real woman.

So forget that you live with your three under-fives on the eleventh floor of a tower block with no working lift. Don't worry that you are claiming benefits because you have no childcare and so can't go out to work. If you want to, just go and run for prime minister. Or don't. Either way, you are empowered. If the idea of public office feels too cumbersome, then choose to turn your attention to your armpits. To shave or not to shave? It's your choice, remember.

Those with power never talk about 'empowerment' in relation to themselves because they don't need to. Multi-millionaire Watson showed her true colours when betraying the most disenfranchised women, such as those in prison, domestic violence refuges or hospital wards, when she declared that 'trans-women are women' and should be treated as such. This means, following its logical conclusion, that women-only spaces become a thing of the past.

Following *Harry Potter* creator JK Rowling's critiquing of extreme transgender ideology, Watson tweeted, 'Trans people are who they say they are and deserve to live their lives without being constantly questioned or told they aren't who they say they are.'

Watson's remarks were clearly in response to Rowling expressing concern about young women, in particular lesbians, latching on to the idea of transitioning as a way to escape the hell of womanhood, and in particular, the context of sexualisation and harassment girls are raised within.

It is perfectly fine for Watson to hold the belief that trans women are women, and understandable that her legion of young, primarily female fans consider her a role model and therefore will be influenced by her views. But whilst Rowling is besmirched and dismissed as 'transphobic' despite having never expressed an anti-trans sentiment, all Watson is required to do to be on the receiving end of copious praise is to repeat the Stonewall mantra.

In this instance, Watson's self-serving narcissism shone through as clearly as Rowling's integrity.

The kind of choice feminism that Watson spouts has its roots in the most privileged ideology imaginable. It is not dissimilar to Margaret Thatcher's 'pull yourself up by your bootstraps' attitude and shows zero awareness of the constraints on so many real women's lives. In the same way that Emma thinks men can identify themselves into being women, she somehow thinks that women with nothing can 'empower' themselves to become world leaders. That might have been how it worked for Watson but that's not feminism.

When choice bites back

The 'choices' that women make about being choked, being 'sex workers', hoping for a white wedding and so on are all taken out of context and seen as individual lifestyle choices. If you dismiss the solidarity between women and our common oppression, then what responsibility do any of us have to one another as women? We can only have feminism if we address the reality of women's oppression as it affects all women.

Choice feminists prioritise the individual and name any choice a woman makes as a feminist one, simply because a woman is making it. Everyone wants choice. But women have been denied a choice for so long that many now define such basic life markers as being able to choose whether or not to marry, to have children, or which career to pursue as feminism itself. Things as basic as this are being mistaken for feminism and saying 'it's my choice' effectively disables any discussion about sexist institutions. It is deeply unhelpful.

If we continue to think about issues like pornography, prostitution, sexual practice from men towards women, heterosexual relationships, merely as a matter of individual choice, we fail to understand one of the most fundamental mechanisms by which women are oppressed, which is the control of women's bodies by men. These are issues that are hugely significant in terms of how women are controlled.

And if feminism is about choice, what does this mean for the women and girls who don't have any choice? The girls forced into marriage, the women pimped out by violent boyfriends, the women on benefits living in temporary accommodation with young children they can't afford to feed. For feminism to mean anything, it has to be for all women and not just the privileged few.

The fight to choose?

A crucial women's liberation slogan in early second-wave feminism was 'Abortion – a woman's right to choose'. Access to contraception and abortion meant it was suddenly possible to choose if and when to have children. But the argument from neoliberals now is: how can you support a woman's right to choose and to take control over her reproductive system when you deny her the right to engage in 'sex work'?

In a *New Statesman* article entitled 'From abortion to sex work, why the state shouldn't control women's bodies', Frankie Mirren writes: 'Behind the opposition to decriminalise both abortion and sex work lies the belief that some people . . . are incapable of physical autonomy, that their choices are so socially harmful, so deluded, they must be legislated against.'

What Mirren says seeks to position feminists who critique the sex trade as 'anti-choice', which suggests that to be against prostitution is to be against women's bodily autonomy and therefore reproductive rights. It also suggests that those feminists are prudish anti-sex moralists.

Jo Costello, a working-class feminist, works at a women's refuge in the north-east of England. She is enraged by the way some middle-class progressives consider prostitution to be a choice and work. In her view, 'Until prostitution is offered as a career choice at Cheltenham Ladies' College, then it's obvious they mean we should be selling blow jobs on Hartlepool harbour for five pounds. The posh kids are allowed to have proper careers and leave the dross for us.'

As feminist and sex-trade survivor Fiona Broadfoot says, 'Prostitution takes away every bit of a woman's choice, leaving the punter and the pimp with all the choice in the world.

Prostitution is what is done to women, not something women would choose if they had an alternative.'

Should men be allowed to buy and sell women? Isn't there something wrong with men getting off on sex with women who don't desire them? This is about *men's choice* and *men's freedom* at the expense of women, and often argued for in the name of women. Yet the tendency to focus on women's rather than men's choices asserts itself whenever there is a conversation about male violence against women. Domestic violence: *Why did she stay?* Rape: *What was she wearing?* The 'grey areas' of consensual/non-consensual sex: *But did she actually say 'no'?* Prostitution: *But what if she wants to?*

Today, human rights organisations that should be concerned with the violation of the most marginalised women are more likely to support the system of prostitution as opposed to seeking its abolition. For example, Amnesty International campaigns for the removal of all laws pertaining to prostitution, including pimping and brothel-owning:

> As part of the My Body My Rights campaign, Amnesty International sought to develop a policy around the decriminalisation of sex work. The My Body My Rights campaign seeks to raise awareness of, and advocate for, sexual and reproductive rights. One of the guiding principles of this campaign is that people should be able to exercise autonomy over their bodies, reproductive capacities, and sexual choices.
>
> (Amnesty International Australia)

Sabrinna Valisce is a sex-trade survivor from Australia, who sold sex in legal and illegal brothels before exiting prostitution.

She used the 'choice' argument during her time in prostitution and would argue 'indignantly' whenever feminists questioned her about this. When volunteering for the pro-prostitution organisation the New Zealand Prostitute Collective (NZPC) she was given the job of finding all of the media clippings relating to the campaign for decriminalisation. She came across an article in which a formerly prostituted woman was interviewed and explained that it was not until she was out of the sex trade that she realised how hellish prostitution was, and that she dared not admit that to herself when she was selling sex.

'I realised when I read that, "Oh God, that's me",' says Valisce. 'So as I started coming across other articles, I started actually reading them for the first time.'

She now campaigns for the abolition of the sex trade.

I asked her whether selling sex ever made her feel empowered. She replied: 'Whenever I was with a punter, I had to push my own sexuality down. If it hurt, was uncomfortable or a turn-off for me, I had to suppress my natural response to recoil.'

In other words, in order to 'please' the punter, Valisce felt it necessary to ignore her own responses as well as control her body language, facial expressions and other gestures. 'I had to pretend the experience was pleasurable, exciting and fun,' she said. 'This is the very antithesis of body positivity, sex positivity, freedom and exploration. It's not even sex. It is abusive by its very nature.'

In 2017, I took part in a debate with Valisce at a UK university about the decriminalisation of prostitution. Opposing us were members of the pro-prostitution lobby group the English Collective of Prostitutes. We won hands down, despite the fact that at the beginning of the debate a show of hands confirmed that the vast majority of the students attending were pro-decriminalisation.

One of the things that turned the debate in our favour was when a male student, in response to Valisce telling the audience that prostitution was horrendous exploitation, told us about how much he hated doing a shift in McDonald's to support his tuition fees. The student said his boss was a bully and that he had been scalded with boiling oil one day: 'How can you say that sex work is any worse than working in McDonald's?'

Valisce asked him if he would rather 'take it up the ass' and suck the dick of the man sitting next to him in the lecture theatre than go back to McDonald's and flip some more burgers. The student conceded that McDonald's would be his preferred choice. More to the point, judging by the look on the faces of a number of the other male students, they all agreed with him.

Prostitution: Who benefits?

Speaking with the student after the debate, he explained to me that it was because he was a socialist that he supported 'workers rights' for 'sex workers' and that his 'feminism' meant that he supported 'a woman's right to choose' to be 'sex workers'.

But given how vehemently these students support the sex trade, how do they reconcile their politics with their leftist and Marxist tendencies? After all, socialist men tend not to reduce any other question (such as working conditions) to individual choice. They don't say, 'Soldiers choose to go to war and so we can't critique military action.' Only with women is individual choice the final word, and held up as a smokescreen for the harm done to women.

Marxists should look at prostitution in the same way that they look at sweat shops and slave labour. But when it comes to supporting 'choice feminism', they put aside any critique of capitalism and patriarchy and manage to justify their own use of pornography.

Oxbridge-educated journalist and feminist Laurie Penny describes herself as a socialist and believes that her pro-prostitution position is a socialist and anti-capitalist one. She says: 'I think sex is not the problem. Sexism is the problem and work is the problem.'

I am desperately trying to unravel this bizarre statement and to understand how supporting the sex trade can be a socialist position. Penny defines prostitution as 'work' which, by her own logic, means that rape is merely theft. Of course, she would baulk at this suggestion, but if selling access to the inside of a body constitutes 'labour' then how does she imagine health and safety provision, decent working conditions and unionisation would work for the prostituted women?

Feminists that critique the sex trade from a human rights perspective are often accused of wishing to 'limit the choice' for those women who want to earn a living by selling sex. Despite the fact that so many sex-trade survivors are indigenous, of colour and black, abolitionists are often labelled 'racist' or 'colonialist' too because, according to sex-trade apologists, their actions prevent women of colour from earning a living through prostitution.

Aligned to the sex trade is the world of pornography, which similarly presents an idea of false empowerment to women. The cool girls tell us they like pornography, that they don't mind starring in their own self-made film to send to their boyfriends, or watching pornography to please him, and that it can even be feminist. At least, that is the official line peddled by many young women in universities and elsewhere. To speak out against pornography is to speak out against sex, according to the rules imposed on them by progressive young men. And as we have seen time and time again, to speak out against sex often leads to feminists being labelled as frigid man-haters, which is a continuation of the lie told to women about sexual liberation in the 1960s. Pornography was viewed as liberating for women because sex was more than just something that happened in marriages.

I recently connected to a group of feminist activists who had been posting some great feminist content on social media. Camila, a student, told me that she had noticed young girls around puberty age posting naked photographs of themselves in the hope that they will impress men and get 'modelling work'. 'The true meaning of feminism has been twisted to mean that sexual objectification is somehow liberating,' said Camila. 'They believe that making porn from their bodies is empowering. That's the kind of feminism young working-class women are being sold.'

And I have heard from a number of other young women, including those in secondary school, about the pressure they feel to comply with demands from men to partake in viewing pornography, and to consent to sexual activity that they dislike.

The rent-a-womb trade

There is more than one way to sell a woman's body, however, as we shall see. Another more recent debate than pornography that has been raging about women's bodily autonomy and choice is over surrogacy. Increasingly, heterosexuals, gay men and even a few lesbians pay for surrogacy services in order to produce children, and 'my body, my choice' feminism has extended to the outsourcing of pregnancy.

The poster girl for surrogacy, particularly in the Global North, is a smiling young blonde woman who kindly offers to carry a pregnancy for an infertile couple. She does not enter into this arrangement for financial benefit, and handing over the baby to the commissioning parents causes her no distress, only pure joy. She is the surrogacy industry's version of the happy hooker.

And there are stark similarities between prostitution and surrogacy; both are populated by young, desperate women, who find that they have no other way to earn a living while those accessing the services of a surrogate woman have class, financial and very often racial privilege over her.

Sophie Lewis, in her book *Full Surrogacy Now* (2019), refers to surrogates as 'gestational workers/labourers'. But is the inside of a woman's body really an acceptable workplace, whether for prostitution, organ transplant or surrogacy? In her defence of the total legitimisation of surrogacy, Lewis uses the same arguments as do those arguing for blanket legalisation of the sex trade. For her, any ban on commercial surrogacy would 'uproot, isolate and criminalise gestational workers, driving them underground and often into foreign lands, where they risk prosecution alongside their bosses and brokers, far away from their support networks'.

According to Lewis, both prostitution and pregnancy should be seen as work because sex can feel like work and a contractual obligation, and pregnancy is often a situation that at times calls for a strike, hence abortion. The ignorance is staggering when it comes to marginalised and poor women choosing to have sex that they don't really want just because they are desperate for money, or to bear a pregnancy that is hard work because they have no other way to keep a roof over their heads.

And that's the point. The overwhelming majority of women sign up to surrogacy because of poverty, and financial coercion is not a choice. The surrogacy industry is simply the reproductive brothel.

But what about those women that do genuinely offer their womb for use by an infertile couple or individual, an altruistic rather than commercial surrogacy? What right do I or any feminist have to say that she should not be allowed or able to do that? As with prostitution, I would never tell women that they don't have a right to do what they wish with their bodies, but I do feel I have not just a right but an imperative to name and deter those who create the demand for surrogacy. Yes, a minority of women do enter into a surrogacy arrangement without being coerced by either poverty or an exploiter. But such women are, like the happy hooker, atypical. Laws and policy are not made for the tiny minority, and laws also send out a message to wider society. The choice argument applied to surrogacy is a neoliberal one, in that those supporting the practice look only at the individuals who benefit directly from it, as opposed to the effect that commercialisation of women's wombs has on wider society generally and women's status specifically.

Framing surrogacy as choice diverts attention away from the profiteers, such as those that run the clinics, and from other third-party exploiters, as well as the commissioning parents, many of whom know fine well the level of exploitation that women undergo during the process. A number of commissioning parents I have interviewed when writing about surrogacy tell me that they decided to travel from Europe to the Global South, such as Mexico and India, because they didn't think that women in the UK would comply with any contractual agreements, such as handing over the baby immediately after birth.

During my visits to clinics that broker surrogacy services, I have encountered some of the most desperate and disenfranchised women, not just in India or Mexico, but also in California in the USA and across Europe. Military wives who are the victims of domestic abuse, left alone to struggle financially, are classic candidates to be targeted by surrogacy brokers.

Janie*, a twenty-eight-year-old white middle-class woman living in the suburbs in Northern California, where commercial surrogacy is legal, normalised and prolific, found herself in temporary accommodation, having been dumped by her husband and left alone with an eight-month-old baby.

'All my choice had been taken away from me,' she told me, 'because he had made me feel like I could never do anything with my life again, and was completely trapped with the baby. When I saw the advertisement looking for women to be surrogates, I leapt at the chance. I'd enjoyed being pregnant, and so I saw it as a way to earn some money for myself and the baby and become independent again.'

The opposite happened.

Janie was offered an undisclosed amount to carry a baby for a heterosexual couple, but as soon as she began IVF she was required to sign a contract that stipulated what she could eat and drink, and what physical and sexual activity was permitted.

'I felt like a cow on a farm,' says Janie. 'My body was not mine, it belonged to them. I honestly had never felt so powerless in my life.'

In the past decade, a growing number of gay male couples have chosen to pay for surrogacy services in order to create a family, despite the hard-won battle to secure legal rights for same-sex couples to foster and adopt children. The quest to create a baby in their own image has led the likes of singer Elton John, Olympian Tom Daley and singer Ricky Martin down the surrogacy route. That seems like nothing short of narcissism.

It is quite staggering that in all of the pro-surrogacy claptrap I have read, I have rarely seen questions about why the drive for your own biological child can become such an obsession. However, I have heard many sentimental defences of gay men renting wombs because they have a 'right' to father children, and of course it would be homophobic not to allow that. But why should men have a right to their own babies? Becoming a parent is nobody's right, regardless of their sexuality or sex. The use of impoverished women's bodies for the benefit and convenience of those that would claim it to be 'their right' is surely an anathema to women's liberation?

What would real choice look like?

Having considered all of the above, you may be left wondering what constitutes real choice for women? It has nothing to do with attending pole dance classes for exercise or undergoing breast augmentation. Instead, it has everything to do with the right to choose not to be abused and exploited by men, to choose an autonomous and self-determined life, and to establish our own priorities as women.

Put simply, a woman's right to choose is not about choices that benefit men. Only when women are truly free from the system of patriarchy can we begin to imagine what true choice looks like.

Chapter 6

Been There, Got the T-shirt: Can Men Really Be Feminists?

'Only when women's bodies are being sold for profit do leftists cherish the free market.'

Andrea Dworkin

Me, me, me too!

Boston, Massachusetts is one of my favourite cities in the USA, not least because it is the home of my old friend and feminist comrade Gail Dines.

Dines is one of the world's leading authorities on the porn industry and its harm to women and girls. In 2006, I was thrilled to be travelling to Boston to take part in a major anti-pornography feminist conference organised by Dines and her colleague Bob Jensen to be held at Wheelock College.

I was completely bowled over by the presentations at the event.

'We are now bringing up a generation of boys on cruel, violent porn,' Dines told the audience of mainly women, 'and given what we know about how images affect people, this is going to have a profound influence on their sexuality, behaviour and attitudes towards women.'

It was harrowing stuff. Watching clips that Dines had chosen as examples of the extreme woman-hating contained within mainstream and easily accessible porn left many women in the audience feeling extremely distressed and vulnerable. Lots were in tears, whilst other women were outwardly angry and talking about organising a demonstration that evening outside one of the porn cinemas in Boston city centre.

Dines read out a few quotes from women who had been abused as porn performers. They described the dreadful mental and physical toll of being subjected to sadistic and violent sexual acts with multiple men on set.

Jensen talked about his research for his forthcoming book, *Getting Off: Pornography and the End of Masculinity.* 'Porn has had a devastating role in defining masculinity,' said Jensen. 'It reinforces sexist definitions of manhood and influences men's attitudes about women and how to treat them.'

Pornography is a multi-billion-dollar capitalist industry, Jensen told the audience, and yet today, much of the Left seems to defend it. He explained that in the 1970s and 1980s, pornography was a contentious issue among feminists. At that time anti-porn activists were seen as aligned to the Christian Right. But since the 1990s a neoliberal perspective has developed which labels pro-porn activists as 'sex-positive'.

Jensen spoke of the women abused during the making of pornography and the harmful message it sends to men that brutality equals sexual pleasure, whether the violence is acted out or real. In a world in which rape is commonplace, this is a seriously harmful message, said Jensen, before ending his talk by urging men not just to stop consuming porn but to become active in the anti-porn movement.

At the end of the conference there was an open mic session where delegates from the floor could make a comment or ask a question. The aim was for those inspired by the presentations to suggest ways forward for anti-porn feminists and allies.

The queue of delegates waiting to speak snaked around the back of the hall. There were five hundred delegates at the conference, and pretty much every man attending – around thirty – was waiting to speak to the audience.

'Oh well,' I whispered to the woman on my left, 'maybe they want to ask what they can do to join the struggle?' And then the first man spoke, 'I, and I think I speak for all the men here, would like an acknowledgement of the harm that pornography does to us as men, and to find out where we can get support.'

The mantra that 'men can be feminists' is depressingly common, with many men claiming that they are feminists and women welcoming them with open arms.

Once upon a time, men were upfront about their dislike of feminism. They would openly deride women who used the label, calling us man-haters, and ugly lesbians. Today, the tactics of sexist men that claim to be feminist have changed. In order to claim feminism as their own, these men have had to change its meaning to suit themselves. There is a direct connection between the views and tactics of those men that openly disliked feminism back in the early 1970s, and those who, more recently, appropriate feminism and wish to be called a feminist.

The myth that men can be feminists has grown in popularity over the past decade and is a reflection of the current state of what passes for feminism.

Feminism was not created for men, its goal is not to improve the quality of men's lives, but it is available to men if they care about the women in their lives and if they want to change. It was always a fundamental principle of the women's liberation movement that any involvement by men had to be in mixed groups run by women.

Feminism must be a political movement organised by women for women, or else it simply is not feminism. Men need to listen to women and use what they learn from women's experiences and analysis of male behaviour to inform their own lives and choices. This may include, for example, to learn about the harm porn does to women and to stop consuming it. Think about it in the same way as you might do regarding choosing to give up meat. It is a small step towards the ultimate goal to stop animal cruelty/climate crisis, but it is at least *something*.

Once a man has begun the process of rejecting his power status, for example challenging other men about sexist behaviour and remarks, and stepping aside from activities such as speaking at a public event to make way for women with more direct experience, it should be incumbent upon *him* to actively encourage other men in establishing their roles in supporting the movement.

Many men on the left who consider themselves to be anti-sexist realise that to openly express their hatred of feminism could be frowned upon by decent liberals and would rather rebrand feminism to suit their own interests.

The young women who dare to challenge them are routinely punished by being exiled from friendship and community groups, often for merely retweeting a woman who has been labelled a 'bad feminist' by men *and women* out to bash women on social media. There are GIFs and memes produced by victims of this craziness that are as on-point as they are funny. For example, there is one of two witches being burned at the stake with one witch telling the other why she was being put to death: 'I retweeted Julie Bindel.'

Ella*, a second-year student at an English university, says: 'We are currently existing in a cesspit of woman hating but we are fighting back. I am contacted almost every day by women of all ages telling me they are sick and tired of men deciding what women's liberation is.'

The left-wing *Guardian* columnist Owen Jones considers himself a feminist ally. But Jones does not appear to be critical of the capitalist cesspit that is the global sex trade. In March 2015, Owen devoted a column to the subject of pornography after it had been revealed that three judges had been sacked, and a fourth had resigned, for watching porn on computers in court buildings.

'None of it was illegal but they were still publicly embarrassed and dismissed,' wrote Jones. '[And] yes, there's clearly a sound argument that judges should be doing their jobs, not getting off on porn.' However, Jones thinks it's still fair enough because, 'all sorts of procrastination . . . goes on in the workplace. Who knows, maybe an otherwise tense judge seeking a quick bit of relief will concentrate better.'

Jones, like many men on the left, does not seem to understand that the sex trade is built on oppression and abuse, primarily of women and children but also of some men and boys.

Gay men are not exempt from misogyny and sexism. Much mainstream gay culture is steeped in misogyny and hatred of women. Gay men are also on the receiving end of threats and

147

violence from heterosexual men, but this does not exempt them from their status of *men* or from their responsibility for colluding in misogyny.

Patrick Strudwick is the LGBT editor for BuzzFeed News and claims to be a feminist. 'TERFs: I heard all your arguments 20 years ago,' declares Strudwick in one headline. 'My mother was a TERF ... I disagree because I bothered to listen to trans people.'

However, feminists *do* listen to trans people. Many of us share platforms and respectfully debate with trans activists. The problem is not feminists' reluctance to listen, it is more that any proposed debate or discussion is often boycotted and picketed by trans activists who, in claiming their right to identify as they choose, say, 'My right to exist is not up for debate.'

Perhaps the ultimate mansplaining is men telling women who can and cannot claim the label of woman. Many of those who hold the opinion that trans women are indisputably women also hold that natal males should be able to self-identify as women if that's how they feel on any given day. So how can these men possibly campaign against sexism if they don't understand that women are a *sex class*?

Circumstances in which women would formerly have risen up and formed feminist groups are now an amalgamation of gender identity, queerness and virtue-signalling in primarily upper-middle-class settings. In less privileged circles, such as the working-class communities in the North East of England where I was raised, there are women who have much to lose by rejecting male protection or validation, but do so nevertheless. Where are the opportunities or the impetus for these women to become involved in debates about individual gender identities, and what good would it do them to do so? The feminism these women are involved in is grassroots – the type that makes real and material difference to the lives of their sisters. Whether it is running refuges, campaigning against homelessness, or supporting migrant women and their children, there is little or no support from men for these feminists. 'I can just imagine a load of mansplaining posh idiots trying to tell these women how to do feminism,' says Jo Costello, laughing, 'and declaring their pronouns. They would be run out of town.'

The role of the feminist ally

David Challen, who campaigns against male violence against women in the wake of his mother Sally's conviction for killing her abusive husband, discovered that he could be a feminist ally but he would certainly never claim to be a feminist. Talking about how he sees men's role as allies, Challen says: 'What can we do to help proceed the argument to better women's experiences? Helping and finding solutions. That's the difference between being an armchair feminist ally and an active real ally who is helping move things forward.'

During his years spent campaigning on behalf of his mother, Challen's eyes were opened to the myriad problems women face at the hands of men.

'Before my father died, I was aware of how male violence and abuse affected women but only to some extent,' he says. 'The difference between a man who's claiming to be a feminist and one who is an actual ally is that the ally will recognise that his place in the world is privileged, and that they have a duty to use that privilege. Some men get frustrated at being the sex class that is responsible and taking ownership of that. I want to try and do something about it.

'Seeing all the women outside court who supported the campaign for the two years gave me a clear sense of how it wasn't just her story, it was the experiences of so many women trapped in abusive and violent relationships. For many women, my mother's case resonated with them, albeit in a traumatic and unique set of circumstances. There are many other women inside who've experienced such abuse.'

Men need to speak out and not simply retweet an article on rape or similar issues. 'You can't just give yourself a little badge and call yourself a feminist,' says Challen. 'You need to actively try and engage other men, confront other men. One minute they are making out they get it, and the next thing they come out with a fucking sexist comment.'

The White Ribbon campaign was a male-led project launched in 1991 with the well-intentioned goal of encouraging men to cease their violence against women and girls. But it has fallen flat due to being all talk and no action, as Challen explains: 'The idea of White Ribbon sounds good. But it's little more than a branding campaign without anything being done to help. To help engage young men, to help stem the abusive behaviour that men are born to understand, this doesn't need badge wearing. You shouldn't need a symbol. It puts a dampener on what an ally for feminism looks like.'

For him, the men that entertain the idea that they can consume porn and claim that prostitution is 'sex work' have detached themselves from reality. 'They see women as a commodity,' he says. 'They can't have their feminism and still think they have the right to subjugate women, ignore things like trafficking, and pretend that women are liberated when it is clear they are oppressed.'

Challen is raising an important point about what passes for feminism in some quarters.

'How can anyone defend Pornhub and claim to be a feminist?' he asks. 'Why is violent pornography anything to do with freedom of speech? How is putting your hands over somebody's mouth, or around their neck OK, with some even claiming it is feminism?'

According to Challen, and I agree with him, some men attach themselves to this type of feminism because it directly benefits them. 'I think it's difficult for a lot of men to readjust themselves while they've lived such a life where they've been at the front,' he says. 'They'll give some things up, but hang on to what they think they are entitled to.'

Yes, a man can be an ally. But how can a man be a feminist in a movement that prioritises women and girls because of our experiences of the world in relation to men? And why would a man campaign to remove his own privilege? In recent years, the cries of 'How do we encourage more men into feminism?' have been getting louder. It is almost always the very first question asked, usually by a woman, at conferences on male violence.

'This is what a feminist looks like'

To counter the accusations of man-hating that feminists face, many of the 'fun feminists' take a break from baking glittery vulva cupcakes to reassure men that feminism will fail without them. The whole point of the women's liberation movement is that it seeks to overthrow male supremacy and liberate women from the shackles of patriarchy.

Take the famous 'This Is What A Feminist Looks Like' T-shirts that have been posed in by all manner of pseudo-feminist men including the aforementioned former Conservative Prime Minister David Cameron: the same man who cut funding to women's refuges and rape crisis centres and who told Angela Eagle MP at Prime Minister's Questions in 2011 to 'Calm down, dear!'

Also proud to pose in the popular T-shirt is the rapper Tinie Tempah, who is known for his lyrics such as: 'I won't miss her when I'm done with her.' Eddie Izzard (who has said she wants to be 'based in girl mode from now on' and is consistently treated as a national treasure because she follows the revered pantomime tradition of gender stereotypes) has also donned the T-shirt, along with a host of men of all political and sexist persuasions, and yet none of them appear to have done anything whatsoever to further the cause of feminism. In fact, some have actively worked against it.

T-shirts have long been an easy way for people to show their support for a particular movement. I wore an 'End Apartheid' T-shirt on occasion during the time of institutionalised racial segregation in South Africa. Is that analogous with the 'This Is What A Feminist Looks Like' T-shirt? I would argue not.

Wearing the 'End Apartheid' T-shirt was simply a way of showing my support for those fighting to end apartheid; I was not claiming to be a black activist in doing so. I can imagine some people of colour being irritated with white people wearing the T-shirt while not being seen to do much else, apart from boycotting South African goods – but I was not claiming the status of a freedom fighter.

Women are treated differently from any other political movement or category. We are told that if we say men cannot be feminists then we are rejecting potential support. But these critics don't understand the difference between the labels 'feminist' and 'pro-feminist'. A feminist is something only women and girls can be. A pro-feminist is a man who supports feminism and the efforts of feminists in challenging patriarchal norms such as male violence.

In Victor Seidler's anthology about the men's rights magazine *Achilles Heel* (1991), it is recalled that the magazine once wrote: 'We were generally sceptical about men calling themselves feminists or feminist men. We were more concerned to learn from feminism in a way that enriched our exploration of inherited forms of masculinity.' If only those men who call themselves feminists today would take this line. Not only have these men not learned from feminism but they seem to have adopted it as their own personal liberation movement and twisted the meaning of feminism beyond recognition.

When a man wears a T-shirt that says he is a feminist, many women go soft and think the man is lovely and a hero. These are the same women who think that whenever it is a man doing a 'woman's job', he is better at it and more rewarded for it (such as 'babysitting' his own kids). That is precisely why we are not asking them to be feminists or to be women. Because they will always think they have to compete and be the best. But all they are doing is wearing a T-shirt and, despite *Batman*, nobody becomes a superhero just because of what they wear.

Doing it for ourselves

Why does feminism need to be a movement of women for themselves? While we recognise that men are not (often)

153

holding a gun to our heads and there is no literal war, the concept of patriarchy means that only one man has to hold a gun over one woman's head for all women to live in a state of fear and subordination. We have endured the assault course of girlhood, men haven't. We have learnt that men are never going to act in our best interests.

Despite the fact that the anti-apartheid movement had prominent white activists involved, it was still a black-led movement. White people were allies but they tended not to tilt it towards the interests of the white minority in South Africa, or misappropriate the language of anti-racism and anti-segregation to confuse and dilute the message. It was loud and clear. However, we have very few historical examples of men supporting the objectives of the women's movement without either trying to redirect it to their own sexual interest (eg during the 'sexual liberation movement' of the 1960s), or to redirect it so that women's liberation serves men's interests (for example by arguing that sex work is a legitimate career). In fact, there are barely any examples whatsoever of men supporting the women's movement in a way that is actually about women's interests and women's interests alone.

Broadly speaking, the type of feminism that appeals to men is the type that benefits men, or at the very least poses no challenge to them, and the self-identified 'feminist' man is very different to David Challen.

This man is big on women's 'agency' and wants all women to be 'empowered'. In short, this man supports all the things that are bad for women and girls and keeps his privilege and power intact. He will lecture newcomers to the LGBTQQIA+ university society, of which he is the President, about key issues facing both women and 'cis' women today, such as the proper use of pronouns when addressing a non-binary person.

The 'we need to involve men in our movement' mantra that is rife in university feminist societies implies illegitimacy in the movement without them, as well as the idea that women are too stupid to achieve anything without men to oversee it. Why would we need men in a movement with the primary aim of taking away their patriarchal power?

We can very easily identify these men by asking this: are they supporting any campaigns, changes in legislation or social attitudes that would, if successful, result in them losing any privilege or power? Unlikely. If men are enthusiastically supporting aspects of what they consider to be 'feminism' to the point that they are pushing themselves to be leaders, then this is a feminism that will never benefit women.

David Challen is once again the voice of reason here: 'I would not call myself a feminist because I don't have the lived experiences of a woman. It isn't possible for me to occupy the title. Feminism needs to be a movement led by women because they are carrying the weight of men's abuse.'

'It's hard being a man'

Male feminist allies may be few and far between but they are genuine and we need them. They are living, walking, breathing proof that gender is not biologically determined, that men are not innately violent, that they are capable of change, and that we can achieve a fairer and more equal society. These men step outside of the boys' club and endure ridicule and marginalisation from their male counterparts. But how do we spot the real deal? How do we distinguish between the pseudo-woke dudes and the genuine allies? And how can we stop women giving cookies to the genuine male allies simply for being decent human beings?

In the 1970s, in the early days of the women's liberation and lesbian and gay movements, groups of men defining themselves as anti-sexist were set up in order to organise in support of feminism. *Achilles Heel* magazine came out of this movement in 1978, and the articles in early editions tackled subjects such as men and childcare/domestic work, women's sexual pleasure and male entitlement, the harms of pornography and how to strive for equal relationships between women and men.

Slowly, the pro-feminist men's movement morphed into a men's rights one. Some of the very same men who had declared themselves to be pro-feminist supporters of the women's liberation movement and its efforts soon began to complain about problems they had as men, such as being bullied by bigger men, encountering homophobia, or relationships failing because of emotional incontinence. This was fine except these men seem to see themselves as oppressed in relation to women.

It also became a bit of a tit-for-tat between these men and feminists; for example when we raised the issue of female genital mutilation, they asked why we didn't campaign to end the circumcision of baby boys. When we spoke of the absolute misery of women's lives under patriarchy, they demanded to know what we were doing about men's depression. In calling for better healthcare for women, in particular reproductive health, these men would start talking about prostate cancer.

Of course no feminist had a problem with men dealing with their own issues, in fact we very much wanted them to so that the responsibility was taken away from women as their carers, but that wasn't what was happening. The men who had stood by us as allies were, ironically, becoming resentful of what they saw as our advantage. They started to feel aggrieved about the fact that we had successfully campaigned for reproductive healthcare for ourselves and not them. The fact that most heterosexual married women would take responsibility for making GP appointments for their husbands seemed to have passed these men by. All of a sudden, the rights that we had fought for and won represented a lack of rights for them.

Patriarchy is a system that works to men's advantage over women, but it also sets men in competition with each other, which creates losers. Men who lose find it easy to blame women, rather than see how the system kicks weaker and disadvantaged men in the teeth. However, it is not the responsibility of women to mop away the tears of the men who lose through patriarchy.

Somewhere along the way, the anti-feminist men's rights movement became the only male voices we heard in relation to feminism. One of the loudest men's rights activist voices was that of the journalist David Thomas, author of *Not Guilty: In Defence of the Modern Man* (1993). Incidentally, Thomas has recently transitioned and now lives as a woman named Diana. He has documented this journey in the *Telegraph* newspaper. In the 1990s, according to Thomas, feminism had gone far enough. Men had been reduced to a whimpering bunch of pathetic softies, dispossessed of their rights by laws that were inordinately biased in favour of women.

The key argument in *Not Guilty* is that feminism had exceeded itself and caused men to cower like a load of scared rabbits, emasculated and stripped of their dignity and rights.

Feminism had apparently introduced laws that took away men's rights as fathers, sexual beings and husbands. As far as Thomas was concerned, women had become the oppressors and men the whimpering victims. The worm had turned.

Thomas was claiming that it was hard to be a man, even though they usually earned (and still usually earn) significantly more than women, because men are emotionally abused by women throughout their whole lives, from their mothers to their wives. This makes men angry and, because they are discouraged from displaying that anger, they carry that fury around with them and are provoked into taking it out on women.

In fact, anger is the one emotion men do get to express, albeit selectively. Men can get angry at their wives, but if they get too angry at their bosses they get fired. Men who claim they can't control their anger at home often control it quite easily at work. Whatever limits patriarchy puts on men, they are imposed by patriarchy, not by women. If men want to remove those limits, they should resist patriarchy.

If men who hate women and blame feminism for everything are bad enough, don't forget that we also have to contend with men who celebrate the fact they are apparently doing feminism better than women.

In 2015, an article in the *Financial Times* named Virgin CEO Richard Branson as a leading 'male feminist' because he gave a little more maternity leave to his female employees than was required by statutory law. But this is the same Richard Branson who signed off a design of urinals at Virgin's new Clubhouse lounge at JFK airport in 2004 which were shaped like a puckered-up female mouth with bright red pouting lips; Branson thought it appropriate for men to aim their penises at the mouth and spray urine into the disembodied 'woman'. After protests from feminist groups, Virgin decided to scrap the design.

This is also the same Richard Branson who, in 2009, defended himself against an Australian columnist who criticised him for using bikini-clad blonde models as part of his advertising strategy. Branson said that what he was doing was merely 'part of the old-fashioned way of promoting products and businesses that had worked for centuries'. Despite all this, according to the UK's leading business newspaper, Branson is still counted as one of the nation's 'top ten male feminists'. If Richard Branson is what constitutes a feminist in the twenty-first century then heaven help the future of feminism.

Give that man a cookie!

Men are often praised for doing what women are expected to do as a matter of course. In August 2019, the Speaker of the House in the New Zealand Parliament, Trevor Mallard, tweeted a photograph of himself presiding over a debate while feeding colleague Tāmati Coffey's new-born baby – a photograph that got tens of thousands of likes and retweets. The story played out on CNN, Sky News, RTE and every major news outlet on the planet and each one of them hailed Trevor a feminist icon and pioneer for equality. Yet all he did was briefly hold a colleague's baby in a place of work.

As if that wasn't bad enough, consider some background information. Politician Coffey is a gay man who is married to a teacher called Tim Smith. They had the baby via a surrogate mother and announced that they were 'expecting' at the Big Gay in Auckland a few months earlier. In 2014, Coffey gave an interview to New Zealand *Women's Weekly* and spoke about how he and Smith really wanted children. 'We just need to find a uterus,' he joked. Except it turned out not to be a joke.

Fast forward to 2019 and Coffey had returned from paternity leave and brought the baby to meet his colleagues. That was when Mallard offered to feed him as Coffey took part in the debate. The responses on Twitter defied belief. Comments ranged from: 'This is the most wonderful thing I have ever seen' to 'This made me cry, it is so beautiful.' Imagine if a natal mother had taken her child to work and breastfed. Further imagine if she was the Speaker and she did it from that position. There would be unrestrained outrage and disgust.

Instead, Mallard was hailed as a hero to women, despite the fact that the baby belonged to two rich gay men who had rented a woman's womb in order to produce it. And the men were seen as heroes simply for being gay and having a baby, despite the exploitation involved in the child's conception and birth. In short, anything women do, men can do better. There is also the issue of 'damned if you do, damned if you don't'. Take the example of Jacinda Ardern who was praised to the hilt when she took her baby to work at the UN in 2018, but heavily criticised for the cost of plane tickets after she made a special one-day trip to the Pacific Islands Forum in order to accommodate breastfeeding her eleven-week-old baby. The message seems to be, 'stay in your lane, bitch'.

Men have long felt resentful for being left out of feminism. In the early days of the second wave, they attempted to discredit feminism in the hope that it would fade away. When this strategy failed, sexist men tried to take it over by claiming to be the ones who needed 'liberating' from women.

But there are plenty of women's organisations and individual feminists that will bend over backwards to make room for men within the movement. Fiona Mactaggart, Chair of the Fawcett Society whose remit is campaigning for women's equality, says she was 'really surprised' when she began in her role and discovered there were three men on the board of trustees. 'I don't mind men being there but it feels like "why?",' she says. 'Women have been pushed to the back for so long, why can't we push them to the front?'

Despite everything I have said above, there is absolutely a need for male-centric activism that focuses on engaging men. But this should not be confused with feminist activism, because feminism should be reserved as a movement by women, for women. The bar has been set very low for men, and liberal feminism has entirely exacerbated this by not only actively fawning over men who do the bare minimum (and often not even that), but also by widening the definition of feminism to mean anybody and everybody.

There is a distinction between men pontificating about their actions and existence as men, and men actually doing something to advance the cause of women's liberation. With the rise of liberal feminism coupled with the explosion of queer theory and gender queerness, the subject of 'men's issues' has emerged as a distinct social movement.

Liberal feminism has had a disastrous effect on men's accountability. Today we have a movement of young women in the form of liberal feminists who are telling men that they can actually *be* feminists, thereby absolving men of any kind of accountability. If men can be feminists, it removes any possibility of checks and balances that men simply supporting women might have.

Men need to be supported by other men to reject toxic expectations and to remove the burden of educating men about issues such as sexual and domestic violence from women. This should be male-focused work. But it shouldn't be a subset of feminist activism because that isn't what it is, just as feminist activism isn't a men's rights movement *despite* the fact that it often helps men, too.

A student in Bath told me, 'For men to truly support a women's movement, they need to listen, learn, change their behaviour, teach other men to do the same, not expect any praise or credit for it, reject almost everything that has cemented their power as men, and stop trying to take the mantle of feminist when it isn't theirs to take.'

The dilution and distortion of the politics of feminism has been massively exacerbated by the rise in gender queerness, where not only are men allowed to say they're feminists but they can also say that they're women!

Masculinity is a significant contributor to male supremacy and, consequently, female oppression. Men need to focus on this and deconstruct harmful sex stereotypes and expectations *but not as a form of 'feminist' activism*. Saying 'I'm deconstructing my masculinity therefore I am contributing to the feminist cause' is not good enough.

'The reason men don't like proper feminism is because it forces us to confront the fact that we need to give up all the things we like about being men,' says Tom Farr, a feminist ally who campaigns against male violence towards women. 'Where there is male dominance, we have to examine that very closely to see whether it is in fact a toxic realisation of patriarchy.'

This is obviously very difficult for men, but I don't think they should be applauded for rejecting these things, or comforted because they no longer watch porn for example. However it is useful for feminists to acknowledge the social conditioning that has led to this situation in the first place. The question for feminists is how to support men trying to change while not feeling pressured to take responsibility for those men.

The same system of patriarchy and male dominance that oppresses and harms women also makes it impossible for men to be full human beings. Feminists do not need men to be heroes but simply to understand what feminism can offer them – in terms of the way that they relate to women and each other. Men can only benefit from feminism by challenging masculinity and if they wanted to make a real leap forward into a world in which we were all free from the requirement to conform to gender stereotypes, we feminists would hardly be standing in their way.

Chapter 7

The Lesbian Conundrum:
Why Rejecting Men Is Such a Threat

'Lesbian existence comprises both the breaking of a taboo
and the rejection of a compulsory way of life. It is also a
direct or indirect attack on male right of access to women.'

Adrienne Rich

Are lesbians real women?

It was a freezing January day in 2001 as I made my way to the
office – a draughty university building that should have been
condemned long ago. I was dreading the day ahead. I was
involved in a research project on rape and the criminal justice
system and waiting for me on my desk was a pile of data on
some of the most horrific sexual assaults on women that had
failed to make it to court.

As I put the kettle on, my mum phoned. 'There's something
horrible about you in the paper today,' she said. 'I've had to
hide it from your dad.'

My mum read the *Daily Express* because, as she regularly
reminded me, 'a woman edits it'. Rosie Boycott, who had been
in the job since 1998, was a co-founder of the feminist magazine
Spare Rib.

The article, which was a full-page spread, was headlined, 'Women's issues can't be resolved by man-haters'. It was written following a debate on the radio between me and the late Carol Sarler a few days earlier on whether men convicted of 'date rape' should be given prison sentences. I said 'of course' and questioned why the word 'date' should be involved at all. Sarler said men that expected a bit of sex after a night out might simply have misread the signals.

In her column, Sarler poured scorn on my concern about rape by suggesting that, because I am a lesbian, I am unlikely ever to be out with a man, ergo will never be raped by one. She then ranted about how lesbians regularly stick our beaks into 'women's issues'. 'Lesbian domination of these [feminist] groups kicked off back in the 1970s, when the streets were buzzing with fish riding bicycles and the ultimately admired woman was the woman who didn't need a man at all.'

She continued: 'As it happens, I would have no problem with Bindel and her kind if she called her group Justice for Lesbians and kept her excellently honed campaigning skills for lesbian issues . . . Bindel's views, Bindel's prejudices and Bindel's voice have no place within the lives of the happy, or even the unhappy, heterosexual female majority.'

A flurry of letters of complaint from feminists was sent to Boycott, of which a couple were published. 'Lesbians have always been at the forefront of campaigning against rape, domestic violence and other forms of male violence,' wrote one woman. 'We have also spearheaded the refuge movement and abortion rights campaigns.'

Doubtless for 'balance', a letter in support of Sarler's views also appeared in the paper a few days later:

'Julie Bindel et al are not going to decamp from the issue of domestic violence because that is how they make their living. They spread their hatred of men and their warped dislike of family life everywhere they go. The radical end of the lesbian movement has long ago invaded the cause of domestic violence. Many of them run refuges, both here and abroad, which enable them to bully and brainwash vulnerable women and children into believing their pernicious rubbish,' wrote Erin Pizzey, founder of Chiswick Family Rescue who had fallen out spectacularly with the women's movement some years earlier.

It took me some time to explain to my mum why lesbians were vilified for being part of the movement to liberate women. Women are the only oppressed group required to love their oppressor, I told her, which is why men get offended at sexual rejection and heterosexual women feel defensive.

My own letter in response to the hit-job on me was published in the *Express* as the last word on the topic:

'I'm sorry,' I wrote, 'I just don't remember snogging Carol Sarler at an office Christmas party! Surely this can be the only explanation for her virulent attack on me and near hysterical over-assertion of her heterosexuality?'

For feminists, the relationship between gender and sexuality is fundamental. All women are required to be heterosexual and to adhere to the rules of femininity and they are punished for not conforming to these requirements, even those who are buffered by the privilege of their class and/or race. Yes, the rules of femininity change over time, but ultimately, they all entail subservience and deference to men. Being proudly lesbian is one of the most flagrant ways of signally that those rules have been broken, and this 'transgression' results in such women being accused of not being 'real women'. As a teenage girl, recognising my attraction to other girls (and complete lack of attraction to boys), I was told I was a freak and that I would be 'sorted out'. The threat was rape. Today the threat would be a gender clinic.

After coming out as a lesbian in the 1970s, I was beaten up, sexually assaulted, and laughed at by police officers when I reported being attacked by a fascist in a gay club and thrown down the stairs. I was disowned by many within my community and told I couldn't look after my neighbour's children when she discovered my sexuality because I was a 'pervert'.

Since then I have continued to witness and experience anti-lesbian violence first-hand. I have been attacked on more than one occasion: physically assaulted by anti-gay bigots, and sexually assaulted by a man who thought he could 'straighten me out'. I've lost housing and jobs as a result of being a lesbian.

One of those jobs was cleaning in a gay and lesbian bar that was run by a straight couple, Jim* and Irene*, and their son Chris*. Jim and Irene had retired from the police service and saw financial opportunities in running a bar for the many lesbians and gay men who had gravitated to the city from the surrounding areas. 'The queers have loads of money,' Jim used to say. 'They don't have kids to feed.'

One day, when I was cleaning the apartment above the pub, Jim and Chris cornered me and attempted to rape me. They were laughing, telling me all I needed was a 'good fuck'. I only managed to escape because they heard Irene come up the stairs.

Around this time I became very active in feminist activism, and the other women involved became my community. Many were lesbians, and through meeting them I learned to accept my sexuality and to feel proud of my identity. Today, it is extremely rare for me, a privileged white woman living in London and working in the media, to encounter the sort of blatant anti-lesbian abuse that used to be an everyday occurrence. But now those anti-lesbian misogynistic bigots who targeted me and my lesbian friends in the early days have been replaced with the TERF-finder generals, both male and female, who hurl abuse and threats my way in the name of transgender rights.

In chapter 4, we saw how feminists, in particular those working to end male violence, are often accused of being narcissistic white privileged women who only want to elevate their own status in society, and that they care nothing about women of colour and other marginalised women.

Those of us who insist that feminism must centre women and girls are constantly reminded of the fact that there exist other oppressed people (i.e. men) who deserve our attention instead. Feminists are constantly warned not to prioritise women because there are other urgent issues to deal with, such as the climate crisis, animal cruelty and police brutality towards young black men.

I am absolutely not ignoring those issues – and nor is feminism – but surely that does not mean we should be prioritising every cause above our own?

First, we were told that women's rights had to wait until after the socialist revolution. Feminism was seen as a bourgeois deviation from the main project. Now we're told that nothing else matters until the environment is saved, least of all women's issues. It is true that if we destroy the ecosystems on which our lives depend, social justice won't be much of a concern. But, in the interim, while we try to slow and eventually reverse ecological degradation, the unequal distribution of wealth and power cannot be ignored, and the epidemic levels of violence against women cannot wait until everything else has been resolved. All of these issues are intimately interconnected. Why is it even seen as a choice between one form of violence and another?

Human domination of nature is, like patriarchy, one of the most persistent and pernicious systems of control and damage. And, for those of us on the left, we have to ask: why is women's liberation always at the back of the queue? We will make little progress on ecological crises without ending patriarchy, or at least helping people see that the domination/subordination dynamic is at the heart of both.

What's wrong with 'women'?

I remember in the 1980s when the term 'woman' was something we had to reclaim as a positive word. Men called us 'ladies' or 'girls' and the notion of referring to women as 'women' was seen as rude and crude. When I became a feminist, I started to use the word 'woman' in place of 'lady' or 'girl' and, subsequently, my embarrassment at using 'lesbian' (rather than 'gay') disappeared. We still have to proudly claim the word 'woman' but now it is more like reclaiming it from trans activists than convincing paternalistic sexists that the word is not an insult.

In a *Guardian* film exploring bisexuality, journalist Owen Jones asks one of the female participants (who identifies as non-binary) what the label means to them. 'In my life I've come out as a lesbian,' they reply. 'I've come out as a gay man at one point.' This person identifies as non-binary and bisexual and had been told by well-meaning people that: 'We daren't say bi any more because it's transphobic.' Jones muses: 'It's quite exhausting isn't it, having to constantly justify your own existence?' But I didn't see anyone having to justify their existence, only somebody deciding they can identify as whoever and whatever they wish as the mood takes them.

The logic behind bisexuality becoming a taboo label is the fact that gender has replaced sex. Therefore the 'sex' bit of 'bisexuality' means that a bisexual is attracted to both sexes. Men and women. I can see why, for a non-binary trans bisexual this might mean trouble. Surely the only acceptable sexual (or rather gender) identity of preference that is acceptable is now 'pangender'? (I know, it's very confusing. This description is from Bisexuality.wikia.org: 'Pangender is a term for people who feel that they cannot be labelled as male or female in gender. As such it has a great deal of overlap with genderqueer. Pangendered people feel that they do not fit into binary genders, instead identifying as mixed gender (both male and female) or as a third gender.')

Because gender has trumped sex, it also obliterates same-sex attraction. It obliterates gay and lesbian identity. And increasingly it is impossible to use the label 'bisexual' without being deemed transphobic by the liberal left because being attracted to a 'sex' (male or female or both) as opposed to a 'gender' is committing the heinous crime of acknowledging that sex exists.

However, the key point is that trans women are not oppressed as women, they are oppressed as trans people. In the same way, bisexuals are not oppressed for their same-sex relationships, they are oppressed when they are perceived to be gay or lesbian. When bisexuals are in opposite-sex relationships, the world knows them as heterosexual.

> 'And yet, for me, nothing says misogyny like defining feminism as equality for all – as if focusing a movement, or policy, or activism on women alone is taboo.'
>
> (Marcie Bianco, 2019)

Bianco is right. Distorting feminism into a movement 'for all' is parallel to the idea that Black Lives Matter should change to All Lives Matter. Of course all lives matter, but white lives are not under attack *as white lives*. Of course we need equality for all, but men are not facing inequality.

What's in a word?

In 1991, I co-founded the organisation Justice for Women with the intention of exposing the endemic sexism and injustice faced by women as both defendants and victims in the courts. However, our name is frequently transposed in error as Women for Justice, which transforms its meaning. Women for Justice means that women will seek justice for all, whereas Justice for Women means we will demand it for ourselves. The organisation's name is also an important acknowledgement that as women we suffer injustice.

Women make up just over half the planet's population and yet we are still frequently described as a minority group. But why is this? The Women's Liberation Movement came to exist partly in response to the fact that women were, and to an extent still are, excluded from left politics. Yet within the left there are certain groups of women who are told that their issues are a distraction from, or an embarrassment to, the feminist movement. And the reason for this is that women's issues are often rather unappealing for men. This is in no small part because male supremacy is the very problem we need to tackle.

In considering how women are being pushed out of our own movement it might be useful to look at the treatment of lesbians both at the beginning of the Women's Liberation Movement as well as today.

In September 2019, a group of feminist activists in Leeds organised a Lesbian Strength march. Over the years, Pride (formerly known as Gay Pride, which in and of itself excluded lesbians) had become a hostile environment for many women and appeared to be more inclusive of heterosexual kinksters than lesbians. The march was advertised in the local council newsletter *Leeds Inspired*. Months earlier, Leeds City Council had circulated a memo to all staff in 2019 informing them that any residents in the city could formally register a 'gender change' by making a single phone call, with no need to offer any medical or legal proof to back this up. According to the memo this was to 'help trans customers access services quicker and easier'.

A local councillor wrote to the newsletter to express her dismay that the Lesbian Strength march had been advertised on its pages. She wrote: 'This is an event organised by a transphobic group. You can see on their Eventbrite that they are using the terms "Adult Human Female", which is a rallying cry for "gender-critical" (transphobic and trans-exclusive) activities.' The advertisement was subsequently pulled by

Leeds City Council but the Lesbian Strength march took place and was a huge success. This was despite a number of protesters who turned up with trans flags and shouted abuse at the lesbians.

The march was in response to what the organisers saw as lesbian erasure by organisers of Pride parades. Trans people, gay men and queer-identified individuals dominated the events while lesbians were pushed to the back. But those who took offence at lesbians organising their own event denied any such marginalisation: 'Mainstream, high-profile lesbians like the editors of *Diva* magazine and the leadership of Stonewall are clear that trans-inclusivity is not erasing lesbians at all,' wrote the councillor who had attempted to get the event cancelled.

But *Diva* has been heavily criticised for its stance on the definition of 'lesbian' by a number of women. For example, in a list compiled by the magazine to celebrate Lesbian Visibility Week, several natal males were included such as Jane Fae who, as John Ozimek, campaigned for fewer legal restrictions on hardcore porn. Fae is a trans woman who once described 'feeling like a woman' as being 'very feminine and sensitive'. Fae added: 'I like doing traditionally female activities such as cleaning, ironing, cooking and washing up.'

According to *Diva*, the description 'lesbian' can apply to natal males who are attracted to women but define as women. In other words, lesbians can have penises and straight men can be lesbians. When I said this to the editor Linda Riley during a BBC Radio 4 *Woman's Hour* debate, Riley told me that I was 'really transphobic' and that she wanted the magazine to be 'inclusive'.

Stonewall was the organisation that adopted and popular-ised the mantra 'trans-women are women' and uses the strapline 'Acceptance without exception'. One of its ambassadors is Alex Drummond, who describes himself as a trans woman and a lesbian. Drummond, who goes into schools to speak with young people about lesbian identity and issues, has a full beard and discovered he was really a woman after doing a gender studies course at university. In one interview, Drummond describes how he likes tinkering with car engines and reassures us that when he is fixing his car and gets his hands dirty 'that doesn't take away my femininity. Women are allowed to fix cars, too.'

At a time when Stonewall could have begun focusing on the needs of lesbians, it instead chose to prioritise trans women. All of this comes back to the title of this book: *Feminism for Women*. Stonewall has always prioritised men. Now they are prioritising natal men over gays and lesbians. 'I certainly draw out the inner lesbian in women,' said Drummond when asked how 'other' women react to him. This is a whole new level of appropriation.

Until tennis champion Martina Navratilova came out in 1981, there were no positive role models for lesbians whatsoever. She was an out lesbian when almost nobody in the public eye was. Yet when she came out, she promptly lost all of her lucrative sponsorship deals. I remember hearing people refer to her as a 'freak' and 'like a man' when she played at Wimbledon against more conventionally feminine players.

As Navratilova said when I interviewed her in 2010: 'It's harder for women to come out than it is for men.' She is right. It is harder for women to resist compulsory heterosexuality. Women's lives are curtailed by sexism, and openly rejecting men, especially sexually, is often punished and stigmatised.

And when I spoke to her in 2019 she was angry that her rights as a female athlete are up for grabs again: 'We fought for centuries for women to be able to compete in professional sports and some women still can't in some countries. Now, lesbians who have fought to not be discriminated against are discriminated against for being lesbians again. This is coming from the left and it is coming from misogyny. If you really want to be a woman, why do you want to hold on to your penis? Nothing says "men" more than a penis.'

Lesbian rights are women's rights

The oppression of lesbians is not a niche or minor issue. It is a way of policing all women's behaviour, whether about the work it is deemed appropriate for them to do, the clothes they should wear, the sexual relationships they have and so on. The way society views and treats lesbians also reflects the way society views and treats all women. Women are making a huge mistake if they think they can have women's rights without understanding that lesbian rights are fundamental to all women's rights.

I asked Navratilova what she thought feminists could do in the face of such hostility from those claiming to be progressives, and she said that we should respond in the way we do when we are insulted and abused for being lesbian: 'We are who we are and we know we are right, and we fight for what's fair and hold our ground. I'm not going away and being quiet. We cannot be quiet; we cannot be cowed; we cannot be violent or aggressive or nasty. We hold our ground and just keep educating. That's the only way you can go forward.'

The dawn of the twenty-first century was the point at which we sadly began to need to restate the reasons why we still need women-only spaces and when we began to fight for the rights of lesbians. It is no coincidence that the dawn of the twenty-first century was also the time when the trans movement gained prominence and effectively told us: 'Well, you may have reasserted the right to women-only spaces but actually you've got to redefine what a woman is.' So, while once we were asserting that women-only spaces were vital because of male violence, now we are having the same battle in a new guise because trans women are claiming to be more oppressed and vulnerable than natal women.

A trans woman going by the alias 'Genderbitch' regularly blogs about issues relating to gender, identity and disability and was one of the first trans activists to declare that some lesbians have penises. Genderbitch, who identified as a lesbian, blogged in 2009: 'Seriously, if you're attracted to women, then that means you're attracted to *women*. Not vaginas. Not tits. Being attracted to individuals with vaginas and tits is fine.'

Okay, that is a view I suppose. But Genderbitch then went on to outline how one is supposed to behave if one does not wish to have sex with someone: 'There's nothing wrong with simply saying to someone, "You're not my type". You're not obligated to explain why and I know that I wouldn't hold it against you for not finding my genitals physically attractive. Anyone that does is being fairly fucking unreasonable. But don't couch it as "Well, I'm a lesbian, I don't like people with penises." Yeah, that's fucking cissexist as hell.'

Let's try to unpick this, shall we? Lesbians are allowed to reject sexual advances from a trans woman, who may or may not happen to have a penis, on the grounds that the lesbian is not sexually attracted to the trans woman. The lesbian is transphobic and indeed 'cissexist' if she rejects the trans woman on the grounds that she has a penis. However, 'cissexism' is used to describe 'transphobia' by a natal woman towards a trans woman (aka a natal male), so effectively this removes the right of women to name and define sexism *by men*.

Genderbitch's blog marked the beginning of what came to be known as the 'cotton ceiling' debacle. The term was coined on social media by Drew DeVeau, a trans activist and porn performer, to describe the difficulties faced by men who identify as 'trans lesbians' to be accepted as a 'real lesbian' after finding that lesbians were reluctant to choose people with penises as sexual partners. It is a riff on the term 'glass ceiling', which describes the invisible barrier women face in the workplace. However, 'cotton ceiling' refers to underwear: in other words, the 'barrier' faced by trans women when seeking a female sexual partner.

Bypassing men

Women are rarely seen as a priority even by some feminists. This de-prioritisation comes directly from the patriarchy. The first time I noticed how men barely think of us as human unless we are attached to one of them was in the early 1980s when I was a newly emerged feminist living in Leeds. The Women against Violence against Women group I was involved in had organised a fundraising event in a large venue, upstairs from the bar that served members of a trades' union. In other words, men. Because the bar upstairs was heaving with women, I decided to brave the bar downstairs. And as I pushed through a throng of men, I heard one of them ask his mate: 'What's going on upstairs? There are at least three hundred women, all on their own!'

When women are perceived to be lesbians, that's even more of a threat to men because they think they are bypassed. A few years ago, I went out for a celebratory dinner with my partner and another lesbian couple. We decided to push the boat out and went to a very grand restaurant that boasts impeccable service and classic French cooking. The first thing that the maître d' said as he showed us to our table was: 'Where are your men?' When nobody answered, he tried again: 'Are they watching the football?' I politely informed him that 'There are no men' and asked for the menus.

Our service declined rapidly, and one of the male waiting staff was heard clearly referring to us as 'cunts' towards the end of dinner, despite the fact that we had been polite and courteous all evening. Obviously, groups of women dining together is nothing unusual. But instead of smiling prettily or giggling coyly when the waiter asked us twice where our men were, we were obviously mildly displeased and more or less said 'We don't have any men in our lives'. That's often all it takes for men to get angry with women who might be lesbians. We think of men as reacting like arseholes when they are rejected by specific women they are hitting on. But this is about men feeling rejected over the concept of being rejected in the abstract. Had we been a hen party all would have been well.

Similarly, women moving through the world on their own, with neither man nor woman by their side, are often treated as though there is something wrong with us. I travel a lot for my work and often have dinner by myself, which I enjoy.

In 2019, I was working in Rome and went into a half-empty restaurant near the city centre and asked for a table for one. The male waiter gave me the filthiest look and made a big deal out of finally assigning me the worst table in the restaurant, next to the toilets. I politely asked if I could be moved to another small table but was told that a couple might come in and would be more deserving of the better table. I chose not to challenge this and instead ordered a bottle of red wine. I had planned on being there at least a couple of hours and having a long, leisurely meal while reading my book. I was told by the waiter that a full bottle was 'too much for a lady' and he offered to bring me a glass of wine instead. I put on my coat, left and took my custom elsewhere.

Women on their own or women together are a threat to many men because they are so used to policing our behaviour, whether consciously or subconsciously. For some, the term 'lesbian' means only sexual identity. The minute we say, 'Ellen DeGeneres is a lesbian' we're really saying, 'Ellen DeGeneres leads an alternative lifestyle/has a female partner'. When I came out in 1977, I initially said I was bisexual in order to avoid the word 'lesbian'. I perceived 'bisexual' to be more inclusive of men. 'Gay' was a softer and more gentle term than 'lesbian' because 'lesbian' had only ever been used to describe women who were considered to be oversexed deviants. It was only as a result of the gay liberation and women's liberation movements that we began to have pride in our identity. But now we've gone full circle and same-sex-attracted women are expected to identify as 'queer', 'non-binary' or even as trans men. In fact, as anything except 'lesbian', which is used as little as possible.

So long as we have to keep fighting for the definition of what it means to be a woman, then the term 'lesbian' is always going to be lagging behind. Fundamentally, being a woman should be about prioritising women in every aspect of life. But today, rather than call a group of women 'women', we are collectively termed 'guys' to be more inclusive. Most people don't seem to understand the insidious, seeping, corrosive rot that their mis-use of language causes.

As a journalist, one of my undercover investigations involved travelling to a small town in Colorado, USA, ostensibly to be 'cured' of my lesbianism. The conversion therapy was in a Christian counselling centre in the middle of nowhere. I based my character on a woman I had met in the UK many years before called Mary. She had been rejected by her religious parents and her church when she was discovered to be a lesbian in her late teens. Consequently, for many years, Mary battled with depression and anxiety because of the appalling bigotry she endured.

My therapist Kelly attempted to tell me that something traumatic must have happened earlier in my life to have caused me to become a lesbian and that she believed I was broken. She told me she considered it an honour to help put me back to how God intended: i.e. heterosexual. Kelly told me that my lesbianism was because I must have been frightened of my father when I was a child and that I now see all men as scary. Then she suggested that my mother must have neglected me, which had caused me to seek love in women's arms.

In the final session, I asked Kelly whether I should access 'gay-affirming' therapy that would make me feel better about being a lesbian, rather than pursue a route that would end with me losing my existing identity and support network. But Kelly did not refer me to any of the UK's many gay-friendly churches or suggest 'gay-affirming therapy' to help me come to terms with my sexuality. She simply insisted that I must be healed.

Policing lesbians: policing women

The publication of a booklet, *Love Your Enemy? The Debate Between Heterosexual Feminism and Political Lesbianism* in 1981 coined a new label – 'political lesbianism' – which has come to be one of the most misunderstood terms relating to sexual identity. Although the pamphlet gave the impression to many heterosexual women that they were being marched into lesbianism whether or not they were attracted to women, that certainly wasn't the way I understood it.

I was not born fancying the midwife. Lesbianism is a sexual orientation, not a genetic condition. That doesn't mean that sexual preference is not experienced as a strongly felt emotion and a clearly directed desire – it can be. But conservative gay men do tend to insist upon the 'born this way' explanation for homosexuality. Heterosexuals willingly accept this explanation because their sexuality can still be seen as the default position, as the norm, and religious people can allow themselves to be sympathetic to gays and lesbians because we are 'the way God intended' and cannot possibly be changed.

Many lesbians are also keen to ascribe a genetic predisposition to their sexuality. I think it is because the shame and stigma of lesbianism means it's far easier to say 'we can't help it' than broadcast the truth of the matter, which is that it is a greatly preferable kind of relationship – a sexuality of equality after all – extremely enjoyable and highly recommended.

Since coming out as a lesbian at the age of fifteen, I have seen the world change for the better.

In the 1970s and 1980s, there were very few public role models and the depiction of lesbians was hardly flattering.

Butch, predatory and deeply unattractive, these images served as a warning to women not to 'cross over to the dark side'.

Lesbians in the UK have fought for and achieved legislative equality with heterosexuals. We can now marry, adopt and foster children, and have next-of-kin rights with a same-sex partner. It is now illegal to fire us from our jobs or refuse to sell us goods and services on the grounds of our sexuality.

However the story is not the same elsewhere. The ugly, often deadly, anti-gay bigotry in Uganda is often cited by the international human rights community and the liberal media regularly reports on the latest atrocity to befall gay men in that country. But lesbians are rarely mentioned in reports about homophobic violence.

Freedom and Roam Uganda (FARUG) is the only group for lesbians in Kampala and is run on feminist principles: the understanding that the subservient role of women and girls in East African societies is the reason that lesbians face such extreme violence and oppression. 'For gay men, the effects of homophobia are extreme,' says Programmes Officer Gloria Mutyaba. 'But they have the advantage of being a male in a patriarchal culture.' She tells me that lesbians face the most stigma, discrimination and violence because the world sees them as men, yet 'the biggest number of LGBT activists in Uganda are women'.

The dehumanising of lesbians in Uganda is shocking and disturbing. Mutyaba told me about a survey FARUG organised that was directed at health providers and addressed the specific needs of lesbians. One clinician responded by saying: '[I do not] care if these people don't get medical attention. Nobody needs them in the community and I wish they would start to die one by one until they are all finished.' She added: 'The stigma faced by this group made it almost impossible to access appropriate health-care. Which leads to a risk of living with untreated illnesses.'

'Despite the fact that lesbians built this movement, we are seen as irrelevant compared to men and trans women,' says Mutyaba. 'In the same way as women are devalued, lesbians are seen as the poor relative.'

Brazil is often hailed as a great place to be gay. For many years it marketed itself as the world capital of gay tourism and millions of same-sex couples flocked to São Paulo and Rio de Janeiro on holiday every year. The election of far-right president and proud homophobe Jair Bolsonaro in 2019 put a spanner in the works, but even before this, lesbians in Brazil did not enjoy the same freedom as gay men. Between 2014 and 2017, murders of lesbians in Brazil increased by almost 25 per cent and the majority of the victims were young and black.

Milena Peres is a twenty-five-year-old lesbian and part of the team of researchers in Brazil that is investigating the murders and suicides of lesbians. Peres came out in her early teens and struggled as a consequence: 'I suffered abuse from my family, school colleagues and people in general,' she told me over Skype in 2019.

According to her: 'The murder or suicide of a lesbian plays the social role of frightening other lesbians, demoralising and devaluing the lesbian existence, as well as enhancing men's power over the lives and deaths of women.' She added that if a lesbian is raped, it will be recorded as a rape only and not as a specific hate crime against a lesbian.

Lesbian activist Cinthia Abreu, who also lives in Brazil, says that the murders of lesbians, which she refers to as 'lesbocide' almost always involve extreme cruelty, such as beheading, impaling and burns. 'These are extremely violent crimes.'

In 2019, in my home city of London, two lesbians were badly beaten up on a bus by a group of men when they refused to kiss in front of them. The image of the bloodied, distressed women attracted international media attention, but violence from members of the public is commonplace for lesbians in England. That same year in the north of England, eighteen-year-old Ellie-Mae Mulholland was beaten by a gang of men who warned her: 'You and your girlfriend are going to get it ten times worse next time.'

Despite the support that lesbians have given gay men over issues such as the age of consent campaign, and during the AIDS pandemic, the favour is rarely returned. In fact, some gay men have contributed to the culture of aggression and contempt toward lesbians in the UK. For instance, at Manchester Pride in 2018, one of the organisers said of a small group of lesbians who were demanding better representation and inclusivity at Pride events, that they should be dragged off by their 'saggy tits'.

The experience of being a lesbian is, sadly, often the best illustration of men's general attitudes towards women. Lesbians are not an exception to women's experiences, instead they epitomise the experience of women as a whole. Indeed, the perceived insult of being called a lesbian is only levelled against women who don't conform to the behaviour that men desire. For example, any woman who is doing a job that was traditionally done by a man, who doesn't shave her legs, who drinks pints of beer in the pub with another woman and so on, is dismissed as a lesbian regardless of her actual sexual preferences.

Men's way of policing women's behaviour is by accusing them of being lesbians. And the reason heterosexual women are frightened of being called a lesbian is because they are worried men will no longer desire them. If a heterosexual woman doesn't behave like a stereotypical woman, she is automatically seen to behave like a man. Which means that she behaves sexually like a man, either by having sex with women or by having sex with as many men as she wants. It is hard to know which is viewed as a worse crime in the eyes of a man.

Journalist Katie Herzog, who is in her thirties and describes herself as a butch lesbian, tells me: 'I have managed to live a life that is remarkably free of men. It's been that way forever. A lot of lesbians would have been in that position until a few years ago when all of our friends turned into men.' When she was younger, Herzog used the term 'queer' instead of 'butch', but now finds 'queer' to be unspecific and meaningless and realises that she initially used 'queer' to describe herself because lesbians were looked down on in the 'progressive' community in Seattle, where she lives. 'Anybody can be queer,' says Herzog. 'You don't have to be the slightest bit same-sex-attracted to be queer and I now reject that term for myself and I re-embrace the idea of being a lesbian and being butch.'

Lucy Masoud grew up as a lesbian in Libya, and tells me that she felt more accepted in 1994 when she arrived in Portsmouth aged sixteen then she does now. '"Lesbian" is a dirty word now, so if you describe yourself as such and don't stick "cis" or "pan-fried" in front of it then you are seen as a bigot.'

What is feminism if it is inclusive of everything except women's sex-based rights? What is it if we are now under pressure to say we are 'cis women' or non-binary or not lesbians or sexless? Has 'woman' become irreparably unfashionable? Is the movement just about gender now? If so, this is nothing to do with women as a class but more about individual identities. This is the epitome of neoliberalism.

Liberal feminism is identity politics without the politics or the identity. If a white man can claim to be a lesbian and shout 'white feminist' at women of colour, then what does the 'identity' bit even mean? If a trans man who's had her breasts and ovaries removed is being told in her LGBTQIAA+ group that she has to shut up because, as a trans man, he has male privilege over the trans woman who is a lesbian, is that feminism?

Basing liberation feminism on the understanding that sexism is a form of structural oppression is why we are aligned to the left. But trans activists are arguing for the same status as those forms of oppression that are structural. But there is no structural oppression involved in trans identities because it is so individualised and fluid. There is no structure to challenge. What they want is victim status and to be seen as the most oppressed group. If natal women are seen as the oppressors of trans women, this means that feminism is meaningless.

For example, as Juno Dawson said in an interview in 2020: 'Unless I try to pass myself off as cisgender, I'm always going to be on the outside.' Dawson is arguing for a distinctive victim status as a trans woman, as well as all the rights that they see biological women having such as women-only services and sex-based rights to protect from discrimination. In short, they want the benefits of identifying as trans *and* as a woman. This way it is possible to convince some people that men who identify as women are doubly oppressed, i.e. more so than natal women.

In early 2021 Dawson was invited to take part in an online event to promote a forthcoming book at Readings Books, a small independent chain in Melbourne, Australia. Readings asked Alison Evans, a non-binary author, to host the event, but Evans had somehow got wind of the fact that I had done an actual live event at the same bookstore back in 2018 to promote my book *The Pimping of Prostitution*. On learning that Readings had committed the terrible sin of hosting a feminist speaking about the global exploitation of women and girls at a packed-out event at which they sold loads of books, Evans put Readings under pressure to denounce me publicly. Evans tweeted, 'I agreed to do this event providing Readings publicly apologises for hosting Julie Bindel. Where is this apology?'

The next day the bookshop put up a statement on both its website and on Twitter which read: 'Readings prides itself on ensuring everyone in our community feels safe, respected and considered. We apologise for any hurt caused by highlighting the work of an author whose current stance is to divide our community.

'To that end, Readings regrets programming Julie Bindel in 2018 and thanks our community for opening the dialogue with us. Readings is committed to considering the work of all authors to ensure our future programme of events, reviews and discussions remain relevant and diverse.'

Despite asking several times for an apology for the apology, to date none has been forthcoming. The international media picked up on the fact that a feminist had been retrospectively cancelled and denounced in the name of trans rights, despite the event at which I spoke having nothing whatsoever to do with the topic, but with male violence.

My book is still on sale at Readings, as are several editions of *Mein Kampf* in various languages.

Chapter 8

Saying It As It Is:
Dare to Stand Up for Women's Rights

'If sex isn't real, there's no same-sex attraction. If sex isn't real, the lived reality of women globally is erased. I know and love trans people, but erasing the concept of sex removes the ability of many to meaningfully discuss their lives. It isn't hate to speak the truth.'

JK Rowling (May 2020)

Blood, pain, and resistance

Reporting on issues all over the world has its perks. Flying back overnight in economy class is certainly not one of them, and I have pretty grim tales to tell about mice and cockroaches in ramshackle hotels.

Watching the sunrise in the Samburu desert more than compensates for all the dirty sheets along the way as did my entire trip to the village of Umoja, a women-only dwelling in northern Kenya, in 2015.

Umoja was founded in 1990 by a group of fifteen women who were survivors of rape by local British soldiers. The women and girls I met during my week in Kenya had all endured the most extreme male violence and control. One woman, barely out of her teens, told me she faced reprisals from the men in her family for fleeing the village of her birth to escape forced marriage. I asked what gave her the courage to act.

'Is there an alternative?' she replied. 'I was dead inside, and I knew that, if I didn't resist, my life and the life of any daughters I might have would not be worth living.'

Umoja is one of thousands of examples I have encountered in which women *refuse* to accept their subordinated status and male dominance.

The day before I left for Kenya, my commissioning editor called me: 'I'm really sorry, Julie, but we had a call from the Umoja village elder who said they cannot accommodate your visit due to allegations of transphobia against you.'

It took me a full ten seconds to work out he was joking.

I had asked Rebecca Lolosoli, the village matriarch, if there was anything I could bring as a gift from the UK. 'Sanitary products,' Rebecca replied, 'as many as you can carry.'

And so, I boarded the flight at London Heathrow Airport carrying an oversized holdall crammed with sanitary towels and tampons. As I settled down for the journey, I had the most visceral memory of school. I was eleven years old and had recently begun menstruating, which meant I had to wear thick sanitary towels which I hated. These were the type with no adhesive tape to keep them in place, and I was bleeding heavily.

Unable to get permission from the teacher to leave the classroom, and too embarrassed to tell him why I needed to go so regularly, the blood soon leaked on to my pale grey school skirt.

During breaktime I tried to scrub out the blood, surrounded by other girls smoking and laughing at me, but the stain remained just as bad.

I had no choice but to turn my skirt around and hold my bag over the stain.

The boys were soon told by the girls who had seen me in the toilets, and for the rest of the day I was followed around with, 'Look who's on the rag!' and 'She's on the blob' ringing in my ears. I wept all the way home, hoping my mum could get the blood-stains out of my skirt. She couldn't. That mark of humiliation remained until we could afford a new skirt the following term.

My time with the women in Umoja swept away my bad memory and I left Kenya feeling inspired and amazed at the resistance of the women I had got to know. My article was published in the *Observer* magazine on 16 August 2015 and, two days later, an opinion writer in Australia named Clementine Ford used my investigation as a peg for an opinion piece on female separatism. She wrote:

> The . . . profile on the Ujoma village was written by columnist Julie Bindel, and it would be remiss at this point not to refer-ence her exclusionary views on trans women . . . Statistically speaking, approximately 50 per cent of transgender people experience sexual violence in their lifetime and trans women of colour in particular face an increased risk of this form of violence. If the point of communities like Ujoma's is to pro-vide safety and self determination to women who have been stripped of it in dehumanising and violent ways, then they have to be inclusive of all women no matter their race, phys-ical ability or chromosomal make-up.

I emailed the editor who had joked about me being accused by village elders of transphobia prior to my trip. 'Parody is dead,' I told him.

Feminists adopted the term 'gender' to describe a material reality – the systematic enforcement of male power - and as a tool for political change. So it is no wonder that those hostile to feminism would want to sabotage the term. That is also why it is so important for us to reclaim 'gender' from the confusion now surrounding it.

Feminism makes a clear distinction between sex and gender. Indeed, this distinction was the foundation of second-wave feminism because it helped us understand that there was nothing 'natural' about femininity for girls or masculinity for boys, but that these concepts were merely rules of behaviour. Sex stereotypes, often referred to as 'gender roles', are what keep women in subservient positions in relation to men.

There has always been some lack of understanding about the term 'gender', often used as a polite substitute for the term 'sex' in common parlance, but since the 1990s (thanks to the likes of Judith Butler and other queer theorists) it has been completely misappropriated and used to mean something you can choose to perform, rather than something society imposes on you. More recently, 'gender' has come to mean quite simply 'transgender' and is often used interchangeably with, or substituted for, biological sex.

Worryingly, in many left-wing/liberal circles, we are now expected to believe that the hijacking of the term 'gender' is liberating for women, despite the fact that it involves ignoring or misinterpreting the structural reality of male dominance over women. Disrupting the meanings of 'sex' and 'gender' seems to make queer-identified people feel radical and edgy because they believe they are subverting 'heteronormativity'; in this context, 'heteronormativity' is used to describe straight people who are not polyamorous, sapiosexual, asexual, aromantic etc. There is nothing radical or progressive about these developments, and forfeiting the political meaning of terms such as 'gender' is not an effective strategy for women's liberation however much it may appear to open up new choices.

Feminists do not think that women are innately better than men, nor that they have any innate qualities or tendencies to behave in any particular way. Feminists hold the self-evident view that the significant difference between men and women is power. We would not be involved in the politics of change if we believed that gender was innate. While trans activists want to multiply the number of available genders, feminists want to get rid of gender altogether. However, feminists do understand how infeasible it is to suggest to any group that they should not 'do' gender, by which I mean create a story about the meaning of sex differences. Women are required to adhere to sex stereotypes or else they can be violently punished. While Judith Butler, who would have it that all gender is merely a performance, dismisses the significance of institutionalised sexism and patriarchy, feminists recognise gender as oppressive to girls and women and beneficial only to boys and men.

As long as women are oppressed as women, we need the term 'gender' to describe that reality. We need to reassert the language of feminism in order to reassert feminist politics in the form in which we believe they will best serve the goal of women's liberation.

Punished for speaking the truth

One of the things that all strands of feminism have – until recently - had in common is the understanding that gender is socially constructed. Therefore, it is strange that the accusation of 'essentialism' is so readily made against 'gender-critical' feminists. The essentialist politics of the trans movement are rarely critiqued; in fact, any critique of trans politics, however careful and considered, is seen as an act of hostility and even hatred. Every time feminists meet to discuss how to resolve the issues of maintaining women's sex-based rights they are met with a torrent of abuse and such meetings are picketed or even shut down.

Women who speak out or ask questions about transgender politics are shouted down or trolled on social media with such venom that the majority are silenced out of fear for their safety, their jobs, or simply out of the sheer misery of being the subject of such deeply hostile and vicious personal attacks.

JK Rowling is the latest high-profile woman to be on the receiving end of this kind of treatment. Here is what she tweeted: 'I respect every trans person's right to live any way that feels authentic and comfortable to them. I'd march with you if you were discriminated against on the basis of being trans. My life has been shaped by being female. I do not believe it's hateful to say so.'

And here is one of the responses to her tweet: 'This woman is complete scum. Shut the fuck up you transphobic fuck. You don't know or love any trans people if you won't even

194

acknowledge their existence. Thanks for ruining the books of my childhood. Just stop talking. We know you're a TERF. You don't need to keep doing this.' (Ben, intersectional feminist)

I find it hard to understand why so few individuals are willing to stand up and denounce this kind of comment, and to recognise which part of this debate is fuelled by vitriol and hatred. Rowling was making a perfectly legitimate point, based on her own experience as a woman, and making it in an entirely respectful way: women experience misogyny and trans individuals experience transphobia. If a trans woman experiences misogyny it's because she's perceived as a woman and not as trans, and if a trans woman experiences transphobia, it's because she's perceived as trans and not as a woman.

What does it 'feel' like to be a woman?

The journalist Laurie Penny is a supporter of the 'trans women are women' politics. Not wanting to be left out of the ever-expanding acronym rainbow despite appearing heterosexual, in 2015 on National Coming Out Day Penny tweeted that she was coming out as genderqueer: 'Hi. I'm pansexual, polyamorous and a genderqueer woman.' Penny's announcement that October gained a lot of traction on social media from her followers and, by a lucky coincidence, came just in time for the judges of the annual Rainbow List in the *Independent on Sunday* to consider their entries for November. As a consequence, Penny entered the list of 'pioneers in the LGBT world' at number 70 (out of 101).

Writing about her genderqueer status weeks later in *Buzzfeed*, Penny pondered whether her young female fans might feel 'betrayed' if she were to admit that she 'didn't feel like a woman at all'. But what does this even mean? As I have said before,

I have no idea what it feels like to be a woman, I just know I am one because of the way I am treated in the world in relation to men. Is there any innate or specific 'feeling' of womanhood? I asked the majority of women I interviewed for this book and no one could tell me what it felt like to be a woman, although they could all tell me what it was like to live under patriarchy.

But Penny sees things differently. Because she has invested in transgender ideology, which relies on a belief of an innate gender and a 'feeling' of womanhood, she thinks that not feeling like a woman makes her stand out from the crowd, hence defining herself as 'genderqueer', whatever that means. The problem with current 'queer' language is that words are used that are not clear or coherent. In her *Buzzfeed* article, Penny proclaimed: 'Feminism's focus on women can be alienating to queer people and anyone questioning the gender binary. But it doesn't have to be.' And there we have it. As I explored in the previous chapter, feminism focusing on women is a problem these days.

A question of biology

Feminists have long avoided putting too much emphasis on the biological differences between men and women, knowing that these will be used against us to classify us as inferior. We have never denied that there are anatomical and biological differences; on the contrary we argue that it is on these very differences that the edifice of gender is constructed.

It may well be the case that many feminists downplayed the role of biology in women's oppression, for fear that biological differences would be used against us and used to argue that women were inferior. We focused instead on the socially constructed differences that we wanted to erase. It is time for us to reassert the fact that as women our biological differences from men are real and self-evident, but not a reason to discriminate against us.

Many of the injustices women and girls face are directly connected to our female biology: such as lack of access to contraception, abortion and obstetric healthcare, lack of research into treatments for female diseases, under-provision of maternity benefits and employment rights, female genital mutilation, forced and early marriage, rape in marriage, domestic violence, prostitution, rape, the stigma and shame of menstruation... the list goes on. All of these happen because we are female, not because of how we self-identify.

Chimamanda Ngozi Adichie, author of *We Should All Be Feminists* (2014) who shot to fame following the publication of the phenomenal award-winning book, *Half of a Yellow Sun*, refuses to accept that biological sex is either irrelevant or unrelated to the way girls are raised. 'I grew up in a world that said to me, "Because you have a vagina you must cook and clean. Because you have a vagina, you should be educated but in the end it's all about the husband",' she says. The writer recounts a story about her female cousin who was very boyish and always being told, 'Don't do that, you're behaving like a boy, you'll never find a husband.' She remembers: 'As a child I thought, "No, she should be allowed to be whatever she is." I don't have a gender identity. I don't know what it is.'

Adichie was denounced as transphobic and a bigot for refusing to repeat the 'trans women are women' mantra (saying instead that 'trans women are trans women') in 2017 in publications such as *Teen Vogue* as well as on Facebook. As she tells me when we meet, she is often denounced during her public appearances by young, highly educated white women.

In a response to Adichie's comments in the academic periodical *Feminist Media Studies*, the author Mia Fischer makes the astounding claim that in refusing to comply with the demand that she acknowledges trans women *as women*, she is behaving in a similar manner to those within second-wave feminism who, according to Fischer, are, 'privileged white women's perspectives and experiences . . . Adichie's comments demonstrate that popular feminism today often emphasises cisgender perspectives and experiences, replicating a cis-hegemonic feminism'. Yet, dismissing a body of work from a black feminist of note because she recognises that women share an oppression *with other women* as opposed to trans women is beyond arrogant.

Similar attacks have been directed at other black women and women of colour in the name of trans inclusion. For instance, Lucy Masoud, who was raised in Libya, was the LGBT representative for the Fire Brigade's Union (FBU) prior to training as a barrister. She tells me that she is regularly called a 'white feminist' and adds: 'Because obviously as a black person I am only permitted to have one chain of thought.' Despite her groundbreaking work in ensuring the rights of lesbians in a profession not known for its progressive attitudes towards women and marginalised groups, Masoud is now persona non grata in the Blue Fringe Queer Brigade.

Following the Grenfell Tower fire in June 2017, Masoud volunteered to be the Grenfell Liaison Representative, a role she continued even after she left her job having been asked to do so by other union representatives because of the strong links she had built up with the community. In 2019, she organised the FBU LGBT representation in the Pride parade to highlight Grenfell and the miscarriage of justice its victims had endured. 'It was a great success,' Masoud says, 'but then the National Chair of the LGBT group complained to HQ accusing me of homophobia, and then suddenly I'm blocked by them on Twitter, no longer the Grenfell rep and have no involvement in Pride.'

The idea that a black lesbian who has given years to public service could be treated this way would be astonishing to me if it were not for the fact that in recent years lesbians have been rebranded as hateful. Indeed, as I was writing this, Masoud called to tell me that she had been banned from a lesbian online dating site for adding 'biological women only, as one of her preferences because this makes her 'transphobic'.

Unreconstructed sexism

When it comes to anti-lesbianism, the 'gender-fluid' thinking soon disappears and is replaced by offensive sex stereotyping. Take the following anecdote as an example.

In 2004, I invited the author Will Self to a memorial gathering to commemorate Andrea Dworkin. Dworkin admired his work and I guessed she would have been pleased for him to write about the event in his weekly *Evening Standard* column. The column, published days after the event, was headlined, 'Lesbians in men's clothing'.

Self seemed offended that the speakers criticised pro-porn liberal feminists as well as 'hated patriarchs'. He then turned his contempt masquerading as curiosity on the physical appearance of the '200-plus' women in attendance and mused: 'How curious it was, therefore, to observe that these women in their neutral trousers and jackets, sporting short haircuts and only the most discreet jewellery, looked so much like, well, like men. It was as strange as if communist revolutionaries rallied wearing black tie and smoking Havanas, or antifascists donned Nazi uniforms.'

Self perhaps wants his lesbians done up to resemble the women in the 'lesbo porn' genre videos such as *Naughty Girls Sharing their Huge Toy* and *Vicky and Lea Need no Men*. But the idea that by rejecting the fripperies of femininity means that lesbians have a desire to be mistaken for men is classic sexist stupidity. Men like Will often believe that there are certain inbred characteristics that make women reject men and turn to each other. This same set of characteristics are also supposed to influence the way we walk, talk and dress. We have all seen the stereotypes of the woman so butch she could kickstart her own vibrator. As explored in the previous chapter, many feminists reject the notion of a 'gay gene' and consider lesbians to be no different genetically than straight women, but the issue of why or how some of us prefer to shop around the corner remains highly contentious.

Feminists are labelled 'essentialist' when we speak out against the 'pink brain/blue brain' concept of being trapped in the wrong body, because we are now supposed to accept that 'womanhood' or 'gender' are fluid. Hell, we are even supposed to accept that our biological sex is fluid. Pansexuality, poly-amory, gender fluid, gender queer, non-binary . . . we are told that these all are valid identities and legitimate sexual preferences. But try saying that you actively chose to be a lesbian (as opposed to being genetically programmed that way) and watch the hostility come your way.

What do the scientists say? Qazi Rahman is an academic at the Institute of Psychiatry, King's College London, who I met when researching the notion of a gay gene. Rahman studies the biology of sexual orientation and the implications of this for mental health, and he believes that sexuality has a biological basis. I disagree with him on this but respect his work and expertise on a number of issues relating to human sexuality and behaviour.

I caught up with him for coffee and asked his views on why so many young women were presenting at gender clinics and being diagnosed with rapid onset gender identity disorder. For Rahman, such huge increases in numbers over a relatively short period of time could be an indication of social contagion. 'Unless there's something in the water, it has to be a cultural or social phenomenon,' he says. 'Just because something is social doesn't make it any less real but what it does do is limit the explanations that are being given to us by certain groups of activists.'

What we are left with is a cadre of activists, journalists and others who won't shift on the essentialist notion that a transgender gene or a gay gene exists, but 'to a scientist or any reasonable thinker, it seems really inconsistent,' says Rahman.

Writer and academic Camille Paglia supports this theory. 'I believe this is a social contagion that's going on. It's not unlike school, with the huge wave of Goth costuming and body piercings and tattooing. It was going on in half my classes. Piercings in their nostrils and eyebrows and ears and cheeks. It was self-mutilation and self-harming,' she says. 'I think the trans thing, in many cases, is a cover for other issues, all the other psychological issues people are suffering from. The trans identity gives them a sense of stability and a sense of belonging and meaning.'

The threat to female-only spaces

A number of female-only services providing direct support for women and their children who are the victims of male violence have also decided, before the law requires them to, that they will work with trans women in the same physical space.

Female-only clubs and sporting facilities are now under threat too. For instance, despite widespread protest, Girlguiding has ruled that boys who identify as girls can join all of its activities without the girls or their parents being told that they are a natal male. That also goes for adult volunteers working with the children and includes overnight camps – which means that trans-identifying boys now sleep in dorms with girls and share bathrooms with them.

Scottish Rape Crisis also takes the line that 'trans women are women' and has opened its service to all self-identified trans women, meaning that it would also welcome men with fully intact male genitalia who merely decide they are women at that time.

'Her penis was erect and sticking out of the top of her trousers.'

Charlotte Dangerfield prosecuting Karen White

(Evans, McCann and Rudgard, 2018)

Karen White is a classic example of why single-sex spaces for vulnerable women have to be protected as well as illustrating how some opportunistic sex offenders jump on the trans train in order to access victims.

Formally known as both Stephen Terence Wood and David Thompson, White admitted in court in 2017 to a sexual assault and multiple rapes and was subsequently sent to a men's prison. This happened shortly after the Ministry of Justice updated its policy on trans prisoners, which stipulated that trans people in the prison system were allowed to 'self-identify' and to be treated 'according to the gender in which they identify'.

So White was transferred from a men's prison to the women's New Hall prison in West Yorkshire. During a three-month period at New Hall, White sexually assaulted two other inmates.

On telling this story to feminists at an event in Sydney, Australia, in 2018, and in particular emphasising the fact that much of the British press referred to 'her erect penis', one of the women said loudly and emphatically: 'The only time "her" and "penis" should be used in a sentence together is when a woman castrates her rapist and holds up the severed member like a trophy for all to see.'

Fair point, I reckon. Putting male rapists in prison with women who will almost inevitably have experienced at least one form of male violence during their lives makes me sympathetic to such comments.

In the space of a decade, the demands made by trans activists towards lesbians and feminists have gone from the request that we use 'she/her' pronouns for trans women and that we accept that they want to live as women, to demanding that we say we believe they are women and we are now 'cis', and the demand that lesbians should have relationships with trans women.

Fiona Mactaggart, Chair of the Fawcett Society, has always maintained that discrimination against trans women is totally unacceptable, but tells me that saying there is no differentiation between a trans woman who still has a penis and testicles and a natal woman 'is bollocks'. Fiona is taking a risk. In 2016, in its report *Sex Equality 2016*, the Fawcett Society labelled me 'transphobic'. The only evidence the authors used to justify this claim was a quote from *PinkNews* (known by feminists as 'PenisNews' due to its misogyny). The reference to my alleged 'transphobia' was later removed after complaints from myself and other feminists. As the feminist writer Sarah Ditum wrote in an email to the CEO of Fawcett:

> 'One may have good-faith disagreements on the issue of what gender is, and how trans people should be integrated into the women's sector. One may disagree with certain statements or positions. But to deliberately cast other women as the "bad" feminists, regardless of their dedicated histories of activism and intellectual labour, and in apparent ignorance of the misogynist harassment directed at them, is unforgivable.'

A question of sport

The unquestioning acceptance that 'trans women are women' is also leading to the rapid erosion of any meaning behind the word 'women' in women's sports. And this is what Martina Navratilova discovered when she tweeted this in December 2018: 'You can't just proclaim yourself a female and be able to compete against women. There must be some standards and having a penis and competing as a woman would not fit that standard.'

The transgender cyclist Rachel McKinnon (who is now going under the name of Veronica Ivy) responded by saying Navratilova's words were 'disturbing, upsetting, and deeply transphobic'. McKinnon, who bullied Navratilova on Twitter long after she had apologised for her remarks, went on to celebrate the untimely death from brain cancer of thirty-six-year-old feminist Magdalen Berns in September 2019, adding that she hoped 'transphobes' would 'die in a grease fire'.

Both McKinnon and Navratilova served on the board of the US-based LGBT sports organisation Athlete Ally (AA), a not-for-profit group which aims to 'create LGBTQI+ inclusive athletic environments'. Yet Navratilova was removed from the board after complaints about her remarks regarding trans athletes while McKinnon inexplicably remains on it.

Navratilova tells me she heard about being dropped from AA via Twitter and was never directly contacted by the organisation, despite having helped to set it up. 'I couldn't believe what happened,' she says. 'If I was a gay male athlete saying this, I don't know if he would be attacked the same way that I was attacked by the gay community.' I ask Navratilova what she thinks of the theory that a penis is a female body part on a trans woman, and she is unequivocal: 'Are you fucking kidding? Talk about an oxymoron. Has anyone ever attacked a gay man for running away from a vagina?'

Sexism within the LGBT community

Gay men's misogyny has often been excused or even denied, as though somehow, they get a free pass for some of the gross sexism within popular gay culture. Referring to women as 'fish', parodying women in drag acts, and the glamorisation of the sex trade, BDSM and pornography has led to tension between feminists and some sections of the gay community.

Sexism has been a problem within the LGBT rights movement for as long as I can remember. Gay men (usually white, often middle-class) have been telling women what to think and how to behave since time immemorial. It is one of the reasons the Gay Liberation Front split in the 1970s, with lesbians deciding to fight for their rights independently. Lesbians were tired of men setting the agenda, talking over them in meetings and not listening to their concerns. So they upped and left.

The author, journalist and gay rights activist Paul Burston came out in 1985 at the time when Gay Pride and Lesbian Strength were parallel movements. Three years later, the fight against Section 28 united the two groups. When Burston joined the AIDS activist group ACT-UP in the late 1980s, he was struck by just how many women were involved. HIV/AIDS was an issue largely affecting gay men, yet here were women planning actions, painting placards, raising funds and risking arrest alongside gay men on the front line.

'All too often, their contribution has been overlooked,' he says. 'They've been erased from the picture. But I remember them, just as I remember the lesbians who invaded the BBC or abseiled into the House of Lords. They were inspirational.'

He adds: 'Gay men grow up in a homophobic world, so it's no wonder many of us struggle with internalised homophobia. But we also grow up in a sexist society, so as men we're also conditioned to think we're somehow superior to women. Some of us are conscious of this and work to overcome our conditioning ... and others don't.'

However anti-sexist the gay man in question might consider himself, the urge to silence women, talk over them and tell them how to think or what to say can overtake the desire to see women as equal human beings. 'The dehumanising words used to shame and silence: "bitch", "cunt", "hag", "TERF". It's the same old story, however it's dressed up. "Woke" sexism is still sexism. Gay misogyny is still misogyny and it's shameful,' Burston says. 'As the woke bros say, "Do better!"'

Silencing feminists

How better to keep feminist theory away from universities, and therefore young minds, than to literally ban feminists from speaking at the institutions? I have been invited and then uninvited from numerous events at universities following protests from trans activists, supporters of 'sex work is work' politics, and cultural relativists objecting to my condemnation of Islamic fundamentalism, to name but a few.

I have also been invited and then no-platformed by the Maltese and Norwegian governments; a number of events exploring free speech; a theatre event about 'speaking truth to power'; a Catholic college in Texas; the screening of a film about women exiting prostitution (my area of expertise) by *The Guardian* following threats from trans activists and 'sex work is work' allies; and had an attempted no-platforming from a debate at Essex University on pornography, at which my opponent, a man who has made money from rape and racist porn genres, was given a warm welcome by the sea of blue – and orange – students.

In June 2019, I was invited to give a talk on male violence and feminist resistance at the University of Edinburgh as part of a panel looking at women's sex-based rights and the current threats to those rights.

One of the other speakers was Rosa Freedman, a law professor who advises the United Nations on human rights. Her talk focused on how changing the law concerning the right of transgender people to self-identify as the opposite sex could cause problems for women and girls. A passionate defender of human rights for all, Freedman outlined the ways in which there could be a clash of rights between male-bodied trans women and natal women and girls in settings such as prisons, changing rooms and sports facilities, amongst others. That was enough for the more extreme transgender rights activists and their allies to decide that the entire event was focused on removing the rights of transgender people and we were greeted by a large protest outside the venue.

The university, having been harangued by the protesters in the weeks building up to the event, had laid on additional security. It passed without any serious disruption, although some stink bombs were let off in the venue during the seminar. But on my way out of the event room, a man I recognised from the earlier protest appeared from around the corner and started screaming obscenities at me. 'You fucking cunt, you bitch,' he shouted, adding that my writing about transgender issues amounted to 'literal violence' and caused several trans people to take their own lives. The man lunged at me, clearly attempting to punch me in the face while shouting, 'You transphobic piece of shit.'

Much of the press coverage, including in the *Guardian*, a newspaper with a staunch reputation as a liberal newspaper, put the blame of the attack on me and the initial presentation of the report transposed a photo of me with the headline as follows: 'Edinburgh LGBT+ committee resigns over "transphobic hate on campus"' and 'University staff network say their opposition to feminist event with speakers critical of transgender reforms was censored'. My allegation of the attack was contained in one single line in the report.

Both the headline and standfirst were changed hours after it was published online following a number of complaints, pointing out that a story which had originally started out being about a feminist being targeted by an abusive protester following her presentation on male violence, had morphed into a story about my alleged 'transphobia' and the fact that I had 'misgendered' my attacker on social media following the incident. My attacker was charged with violent and threatening behaviour towards me and handed down a community sentence. But whenever the topic of threats or attacks on feminists by trans activists comes up we are told that it 'wasn't really an attack' because, as one commented, 'Her [the perpetrator's] fist did not make contact with the TERF's [my] face.'

Unless we recognise that gender is imposed upon women and girls and used as a means of social control under patriarchy, we will never begin to free ourselves from the trap of femininity. Being a woman is a material reality. The job of feminism is to render that material fact irrelevant when it comes to the way we relate to men. A key goal of feminism is to abolish gender in order to remove expectations as to how we live and behave, what possibilities are open to us, what work we can do and what we are capable of in the world.

Historically, men are not known for listening to women; women were put in scold's bridles and punished for talking too much. If trans women are women, therefore, why do so many men listen to them?

Conclusion

The Way Forward

'When we speak, we are afraid our words will not be heard or welcomed. But when we are silent, we are still afraid. So it is better to speak.'

Audre Lorde

'Feminism for me is about women.'

Chimamanda Ngozi Adichie

At the Coalition against Trafficking in Women offices in New York, Taina Bien-Aimé hears stories daily about the brutality and dehumanisation of black women at the hands of the police. She also deals with countless cases of young women of colour being abused by pimps and johns. 'If you look at the sex trade, it's a different variation of the chastity belt,' says Bien-Aimé. 'The patriarchy has always been extremely creative in trying to supress women in various forms. Calling it "choice" and "agency" is the craziest trick of capitalism ever.'

In order to achieve our goal of liberation for all women, feminists need to be able to imagine a world free from rape, prostitution, domestic violence, femicide, child sexual abuse, and all the other forms of male violence and abuse towards women and girls. If we can't imagine that world, then we can't know what we are fighting for. It is imperative that we recognise that male violence and supremacy is not inevitable.

I'm sure that those fighting to end child poverty have a clear vision of every child having enough to eat, while campaigners against animal cruelty can see a world where creatures are neither harmed nor exploited. But what makes it so difficult for women to envision what it would be like for girls growing up in a world without fear of rape? How would it be if there was no such thing as patriarchy? And why is there such a resistance to imagining this world?

Feminism relies on utopian thinking, and this is very easy to dismiss and even deride, because for women, especially those in relationships with men, it is far easier to exist in a bubble of denial about male violence and female oppression than it is to engage in the backbreaking work of creating a world where these don't exist.

Believing that ending patriarchy is unlikely to happen or 'not in our lifetime' can be a handy excuse not to do the heavy lifting of trying to make it happen. But utopian vision is not and never should be a substitute for material change. That is why a vision of 'women's land' – spaces where women live and raise children together from which men are banned – holds little or no appeal for those of us that wish to face the music rather than hide away.

Without a utopian goal political activity can only be strategic. There are hundreds of feminist campaigns I have been involved in or supported where we were never going to win. Calling for an amnesty for women in prison as a result of male violence, for example, got us nowhere (not least because the majority of women in prison have experienced such abuse so the prisons would have been more or less empty had we achieved our goal) but even so, we felt it important to raise awareness of the issue.

Expressing disgust at the reality of the situation, even if defeat is certain, is crucial.

Being bound by the constraints of patriarchy – and male violence in particular – can feel insurmountable, but as feminists it is our obligation to see beyond the daily reality and believe in that ideal world. We must imagine a world that we have not yet lived in. We have to plan for new possibilities, and truly believe that this world can exist.

But when it comes to the difficulty of imagining a world without misogyny and male violence, there are other factors to consider aside from the resistance to utopian thinking. Not least among these is the fact that most women, including feminists, are in intimate relationships with men. And for many younger women, feminism means a way to show solidarity to other people who have individual identities.

Most women dare not admit the extent to which our lives are controlled and influenced by the fear and reality of male violence. But girls are raised in a world in which rape, femicide and everyday coercion are the norm. Sex oppression is our reality. We subconsciously view everything through this prism and it affects every relationship we have, both with other women and with men.

For heterosexual women, looking across the breakfast table at the man they love, their personal nightmare might be suspecting that he enjoys pornography in which women are hurt. It is not uncommon for mothers to worry about their sons being accused of rape. We are told men will protect us if we behave ourselves, but it's a lie and at some level we know it.

In her book *Down Girl: The Logic of Misogyny* (2017), the academic philosopher Kate Manne argues that those who refuse to behave as 'good girls' are punished by men for their digressions. But how does that explain atrocities done to those women who play by the rules? Right-wing women, religious women, housewives and mothers who demand nothing but the honour of serving men? What about the women who have never had sex and spend their lives caring for others? District nurse Lisa Skidmore was a 'good girl', but in 2016, she was raped and murdered by Leroy Campbell, who had recently been released from prison and had endless convictions for crimes against women.

As she slept, Campbell climbed through an open window and spent two hours raping and torturing her before strangling her to death. When I interviewed Skidmore's mother Margaret, she asked: 'Why my daughter? What did Lisa ever do except good?' What could I say? Margaret was also a victim of the same man. When Campbell was attempting to leave the house, Margaret let herself in with keys to visit Lisa. Campbell punched Margaret in the face, wrapped a cord around her neck, set fire to the kitchen and left her for dead. Margaret survived and when she regained consciousness she was told her daughter had been killed.

Somehow, almost immediately, Margaret found the strength and courage to expose the failures in the probation, police, and mental health services that led to Campbell being at liberty to commit these terrible crimes.

How do you come back from something so terrible – Margaret was eighty years of age when tragedy struck – and manage to challenge the system that lets women down so badly?

'I knew the women's rights lot were there,' Margaret told me when I interviewed the family for a magazine article on her daughter's murder. 'I had seen them on the television often enough, shouting the odds about rape and murder and the like, so I knew there was support out there.'

This is the message that needs to be filtered down to younger women who have been told that 'second-wave' feminism is irrelevant, bigoted and one-dimensional.

Many of the young feminists I interviewed for this book asked me not to use their real names for fear of being bullied and excluded from friendship groups – and accused of being TERFs or bigots – simply for saying they had signed up to a feminism that centres women, and that focuses on male violence and abuse.

Some of these women had previously identified as non-binary or transgender men before de-transitioning back to women and coming out as lesbians. If they had been coming out in the 1980s they would have been embraced and validated by the women's movement. Others had defended pornography and the sex trade, while around half had previously been hostile towards those of us dubbed 'second-wavers'. Some had come across feminism in secret online groups of women who shared experiences of being abused by porn-addicted boyfriends or bullied into accepting transgender ideology. But all would now proudly declare themselves as uncompromisingly feminist: the real sort, not the fun kind who focus obsessively on difference and splintered identities.

Real feminists are hungry for change. They tell me how silenced they have been since daring to speak out about sexual violence, and how difficult it is to challenge leftist men who seem hell-bent on defining feminism for them.

So what can we do to advance feminism? We need to recognise it is an active political movement that puts us in connection with women who share our goals – though we need to come off the internet for at least a few hours to meet them.

We need to fight for a feminism that is about women's liberation and not one that panders to men. Whenever we are presented with a new argument about feminism, the way forward is to constantly check, 'Who is actually benefiting from this?'

I am asking older feminists and male allies to stand in front of the slings and arrows being directed at young women today. Not to speak for or above them, but to support and to mentor when needed. To remember that the level of backlash we are currently facing is also a sign of the potential and the success of feminism, because it indicates the anger with which those who are threatened by feminism will seek to defeat it.

As a result of the relentless bullying and attempts at silencing feminists by self-appointed male 'leaders' of LGBTQQIA+ groups and feminist societies, increasing numbers of women are coming forward to support each other. Those of us who are willing and able need to continue to speak out to show our solidarity to those that are under attack. We need to reclaim feminism for women.

Feminists do not believe that biology is destiny, we do not accept that sex stereotypes are innate, and we do not believe that anyone is born to be a victim or an aggressor. Therefore, we are hopeful and we can progress as a movement. We do not suggest that all women are the same but we look at the things that we do have in common. And what we do share is the fear and reality of male violence, and the recognition that we are oppressed by male supremacy and patriarchy.

Feminism is the most optimistic political movement on the planet, because we don't believe that pornography and prostitution are inevitable or that men are innately violent.

We work towards a political goal that is achievable, not some spurious notion of identity.

True sexual liberation for women isn't sliding up and down a pole in a lap dance club but being open to the idea of not being bound by our relationships with men. We need to dare to think about a world in which there would be no stigma or punishment attached to prioritising women in our lives. We need to see that being part of a couple does not need to be the organising principle of your life. It can be a piece of the jigsaw, but friendship and political networks within feminism are what drive our excitement and engagement. This is not about suggesting that women who choose to spend their lives in a monogamous relationship with a man with whom they have children is making a 'wrong' or 'poor' choice, rather that in order to make a positive choice to do this we must honestly and critically assess how much choice we have to opt out of this lifestyle.

To young women I say this; many of you instinctively know that the popular discourse is against your interests. You know that pornography is not harmless; that prostitution is not an empowering choice; and that women's interests and priorities are different from those of trans women. You will not be protected by pandering to a liberal/libertarian/patriarchal ideology which tells you otherwise. You may get praise from the dudes in your feminist society or friendship group, but they will not respect you any more than those of us they try to resist. These men will fist bump you while they call us 'bitches', 'SWERFs' and 'TERFs' but as soon as you transgress, in however minor a way, you will come in for the same treatment.

Your silence will not protect you, but it will render you more vulnerable to the types of abuse you are trying to avoid. Only feminism can protect you, although it takes courage to take a stand on these issues, and I can attest that there is a price to pay. But would you rather have to be passive enough not to upset any of the men you are trying to impress, or face the inevitable onslaught when you defy them?

The Pakistani novelist and feminist Bina Shah is campaigning against the religious conservatism that seeks punishment for women in her country, while trying to counter the creeping neoliberalism that has given rise to identity politics among some young feminists.

'The young woke feminists have started to attack me,' says Shah. 'They will say I'm a bad feminist because I'm older and being older represents authority. They need someone to kick out at. So it's a fine line between being the guiding light and being someone they want to cut their teeth on.'

Author Chimamanda Ngozi Adichie agrees: 'I worry about young women. It's the curse of politeness and niceness, likeability. I like being loved but I don't need to be loved. It's important to teach girls that. I think they are afraid to say what they think.'

Speaking from her home in Ohio, Rose Kalemba, who challenged PornHub when it uploaded the film of her rape, tells me she has stopped being polite: 'Women are being duped. For so many years, we have been indoctrinated by liberal feminism and told that abuse and degradation are empowering. More young women need to be introduced to real feminism.'

Martina Navratilova is one of the many women I have met during my decades in the women's liberation movement who refuses to be silenced. 'My mum used to ask me, "Why do you have to be the one to come out and be public about all of this?" I would say, "Well, we owe it to the younger ones to set a standard. We have to demand our rights. They will never be handed to us."'

Sex-trade survivor and feminist abolitionist Rachel Moran believes that capitulation to fear is the definition of cowardice: 'If there is anything more frightening than standing up to the worst excesses of extreme anti-feminism which masquerades as feminism, it is walking into the future it will create for us if we do not.'

Whether it is women escaping prostitution in Cambodia; taking their rapists to court in India; demanding action from governments to expose murdered and missing women across Canada; closing down lap dance clubs and challenging men's 'right' to sexually exploit us in the UK; campaigning against surrogacy in the USA; or simply refusing to be defined and labelled by men, the inventiveness and tenacity of feminism knows no bounds. Women always rise up. And when we rise, great things happen, despite the fact that we become targets for the boot of patriarchy.

We have had enough stories of rape, prostitution, sexual harassment and other forms of extreme male violence. As far back as 1978, Louise Armstrong described the phenomenon of childhood sexual abuse in her groundbreaking book *Kiss Daddy Goodnight* and linked it to male supremacy in general as opposed to the actions of an individual deviant man.

As Armstrong wrote in 1996: 'People say to me, "But at least we're talking about it now." Yes. But it was not our intention merely to start a long conversation. Nor did we intend simply to offer up one more topic for talk shows, or one more plot option for ongoing dramatic series. We hoped to raise hell. We hoped to raise change. What we raised, it would seem, was discourse.'

The silence has long been broken. So what now? We need to raise hell. The #MeToo movement, like all hashtag campaigns, is no substitute for action. Let's point the finger at men that rape rather than rolling out more women to disclose and lay bare their experiences. It is surely time for #HimToo?

Women need to continue to organise against male violence and oppression, and to do so we need to join forces across the generations. Working-class women, traditionally spoken over, dismissed, parodied and stigmatised, should amplify their voices loud and clear, as should all those women that have been marginalised and ignored within the wider feminist move-ment. But at the same time, it is crucial that we demand to be heard when we speak of what bonds and unites women, not only that which fragments us. In order to strengthen solidarity between us, women must admit to and emphasise our com-mon oppression. We need to name the harm caused by the tyranny of male violence and abuse and join forces to resist and to end it.

Let us build a feminist revolution grounded in solidarity as opposed to conflict and sectarianism.

For feminism to be effective women need not to *include* men but to demand their support in eliminating sex stereotypes and the patterns of violence imposed on women in the name of those stereotypes. We must point the finger at the perpetrators of rape and domestic violence whilst at the same time building coalitions between feminists and those men that wish to be free of the shackles of masculinity as a means to freeing women from the oppressive forces of patriarchy. Had Sally Challen, during her time in prison for killing her abusing and controlling husband Richard, not known of feminism, and not understood that we hold the tools, knowledge and commitment that would lead to her freedom from her prison cell and liberation from the label of 'murderer' she would very likely still be incarcerated.

Had Sally's son David failed to make the connection between his father's abusive and controlling treatment of his mother and the fatal actions of hers which followed from this history, he would not have known to join forces with feminists to campaign for his mother's release.

Feminists have pressured the CPS to better prosecute rape and all other forms of violence towards women and girls. It is due to feminist campaigning that domestic violence, rape in marriage; Female Genital Mutilation; forced marriage; coercive control; stalking and harassment; and commercial sexual exploitation have all been made statutory criminal offences. There is much more to be done, but these achievements came about because of feminist boots on the ground, and a coming together of women under the banner of a common cause.

We need to reclaim the nuts and bolts of feminism whilst allowing it to expand as times and the needs of women change. A feminism for women has to be just that: we have to be honest with ourselves about what passes for feminism today, and who is really benefiting from it.

A feminism for women will liberate, and nothing less should be tolerated. Women and girls deserve a world without rape and abuse in which we are not raised to fear and avoid men's violence. That world awaits us. Utopia is underrated.

Acknowledgements

Thank you to Lee Nurse for massive support with organising and structuring the interview data, and to Jane Duffus for superb editorial assistance.

To Bob Jensen for reading each chapter as it developed and giving me invaluable suggestions for clarity.

Huge thanks to Jess Gulliver and Andreas Campomar for ongoing support and encouragement, and to Claire Chesser for her sharp and concise edits.

My agent Becky Thomas is a mensch. Not only does she never give up, Becky's commitment to and support of her authors knows no bounds. I am very lucky to have her.

My fifty interviewees, many of whom did not end up being directly quoted, form the basis for this book. I am grateful to every one of you.

The group discussions I had with young feminists in London, Glasgow, Toronto and Uganda proved crucial in helping me better understand both the barriers and opportunities for engaging directly in feminism in such a hostile environment.

Without Joan Scanlon this book might not exist at all. When I was stuck in writer's block, Joan encouraged me to discuss my central ideas and themes with her, usually over the dreaded

Zoom on a Sunday morning. Joan's guidance helped me formulate my views, which began in conversation and ended up in these pages.

I met Sandra McNeill when I was eighteen years old, and I can honestly say that without her mentoring, guidance and friendship my life could have gone in a different direction. Sandra has fought against male violence and for the liberation of women for decades, and I can think of no better example of true sisterhood.

My feminist friends spread out across a number of countries around the world sustain me through difficult times, reminding me that personal attacks are part of the backlash against our movement. Without these women, with whom I debate, laugh, cry and plot, I could not carry on this fight.

Harriet Wistrich has been in my life since 1987. I genuinely find it impossible to put into words everything she means to me, but I suspect she knows.

Sources

In writing this book, I have drawn from interviews I have conducted with various friends and colleagues over the years. Words from the following people are taken from these interviews unless otherwise stated.

Cinthia Abreu, Nimco Ali, Lisa Avalos, Taina Bien-Aimé, Naomi Bridges, Fiona Broadfoot, Paul Burston, Beatrix Campbell, David Challen, Jo Costello, Gail Dines, Andrea Dworkin, Kate Ellis, Tom Farr, Linda Grant, Katie Herzog, Claire Heuchan, Karen Ingala Smith, Rose Kalemba, Winnie Li, Rebecca Lolosoli, Audre Lorde, Fiona Mactaggart, David Madden, Lucy Masoud, Fiona McKenzie, Rachel Moran, Ellie-Mae Mulholland, Gloria Mutyaba, Martina Navratilova, Chimamanda Ngozi Adichie, Camille Paglia, Pragna Patel, Francine Pelletier, Milena Peres, Nathalie Provost, Qazi Rahman, Raquel Rosario Sanchez, Joan Scanlon, Bina Shah, Gloria Steinem, Vaishnavi Sundar, Sabrinna Valisce, Ella Whelan, Rebecca Whisnant.

Preface

Feminism Unmodified: Discourses on Life and Law, Catharine
Mackinnon (1987)

Introduction

JB Telegraph article 2003

http://archive.li/1bcWN#selection-257.0-257.183

NGO Equality Now survey

https://www.revelist.com/world/countries-marital-rape-legal/7073/
nations-where-child-marriage-is-legal-account-for-some-of-the-
most-disturbing-allowances-of-rape/3

End Violence against Women Coalition survey

https://www.theweek.co.uk/98330/when-did-marital-rape-become-a-crime

Savile and the normalisation of child abuse

https://blogs.lse.ac.uk/politicsandpolicy/institutions-and-the-banality-
of-evil-learning-from-rotherham-and-savile/

Grooming gangs and 'lifestyle choice'

https://www.tandfonline.com/doi/
full/10.1080/17512786.2016.1164613?src=recsys

Trans rape statistics

https://www.thetimes.co.uk/article/police-forces-let-rapists-record-
their-gender-as-female-d7qtb7953

Martina Navratilova tweet

https://www.theguardian.com/sport/2019/feb/17/martina-navratilova-
criticised-over-cheating-trans-women-comments

Chapter 1

CPS drops 'weak cases'

https://www.theguardian.com/law/2020/jun/30/cps-secretly-dropped-
weak-cases-say-rights-groups

Centre for Women's Justice

https://www.centreforwomensjustice.org.uk/

Porn as 'sex work'

Sexing the Millennium: A Political History of the Sexual Revolution, Linda Grant (1993)

Pornland, Gail Dines (2010)

Pornography: Men Possessing Women, Andrea Dworkin (1979)

Anticlimax: A Feminist Perspective on the Sexual Revolution, Sheila Jeffreys (1990)

Rosie Boycott

https://www.dailymail.co.uk/femail/article-1232485/My-generation-created-sexual-revolution--wrecking-lives-women-since.html

Nagging and shagging defence

https://www.theguardian.com/politics/2008/nov/09/harriet-harman-defence-of-provocation

Judge Hayden

https://www.theguardian.com/law/2019/apr/03/english-judge-says-man-having-sex-with-wife-is-fundamental-human-right

https://www.bbc.co.uk/news/uk-56937149

Feminism has succeeded – so why don't we call it quits?

https://www.spectator.com.au/2019/05/feminism-has-succeeded-so-why-dont-we-call-it-quits/

Fathers for Justice

https://www.fathers-4-justice.org/

Chapter 2

Violence against women and girls

http://femicide-watch.org/

Why Women Are Blamed For Everything: Exploring the Victim Blaming of Women Subjected to Violence, Jessica Taylor (2020)

'Victim feminism'

The Morning After: Sex, Fear, and Feminism on Campus, Katie Roiphe (1993)

Wolfpack story

https://www.theguardian.com/world/2019/apr/23/wolf-pack-case-spain-feminism-far-right-vox

'beleaguered, fragile, intuitive angels'

Fire with Fire: The New Female Power and How It Will Change the 21st Century, Naomi Wolf (1993)

Armie Hammer story

https://www.cosmopolitan.com/sex-love/a35447828/armie-hammer-bdsm-fetish-educator/

Justifying male behaviour

Feminism Unmodified: Discourses on Life and Law, Catharine Mackinnon (1987)

Rough sex defence to be scrapped

https://www.bbc.co.uk/news/uk-politics-53064086

Rough sex defence

https://www.theguardian.com/society/2020/jun/03/rough-sex-defence-led-to-over-60-victims-having-to-deny-giving-consent-finds-research?CMP=share_btn_tw

We Can't Consent to This

https://wecantconsenttothis.uk/aboutus

UNODC femicide

https://www.unodc.org/documents/data-and-analysis/gsh/Booklet_5.pdf

Paris Lees article

https://www.vice.com/en/article/zn7b79/enjoying-catcalls-paris-lees-column

Laura Bates on street harassment

https://www.theguardian.com/lifeandstyle/womens-blog/2014/feb/28/women-street-harassment-power-control-violence

Feminism and class

What Women Want: Fun, Freedom and an End to Feminism, Ella Whelan (2017)

SOURCES

Mike Hancock

https://www.theguardian.com/uk-news/2013/sep/14/yarls-wood-immigrant-sex-abuse-tanja

https://www.theguardian.com/politics/2014/jun/18/mike-hancock-settles-sexual-assault-claim

https://www.spectator.co.uk/article/exclusive-clegg-ignored-a-sexual-harassment-complaint-about-a-second-lib-dem

'upsetting details'

'The Trouble with Teaching Rape Law' by Jeannie Suk (*The New Yorker*, 2014)

Trigger warnings in universities

https://www.insidehighered.com/news/2014/12/17/harvard-law-professor-says-requests-trigger-warnings-limit-education-about-rape-law

Sex-trade survivors

Paid For: My Journey through Prostitution, Rachel Moran (2013)

'Carceral feminism'

What Is Race? Who Are Racists? Why Does Skin Colour Matter? And Other Big Questions, Claire Heuchan (2018)

Me, Not You: The Trouble with Mainstream Feminism, Alison Phipps (2020)

Revolting Prostitutes, Molly Smith and Juno Mac (2018)

Foucault, Feminism, and Sex Crimes, Chloe Taylor (2009)

'Anti-Carceral Feminism and Sexual Assault – A Defence', Chloe Taylor (2018)

Southall Black Sisters

https://southallblacksisters.org.uk/

Deborah Frances-White on #MeToo

https://www.theguardian.com/commentisfree/2018/dec/31/men-metoo-power-women-feelings

Alyssa Milano tweet

https://twitter.com/alyssa_milano/status/919659438700670976?lang=en

Chapter 3

'like moths to a flame' Mike Buchanan

https://www.mirror.co.uk/news/uk-news/mike-buchanan-leader-justice-men-5046517

James Simister case

https://www.bbc.co.uk/news/uk-england-wiltshire-25887987

2014 statistics

https://www.theguardian.com/law/2014/dec/01/109-women-prosecuted-false-rape-allegations

Fawcett Society

https://www.fawcettsociety.org.uk/about

Fawcett Society 2016 report

https://www.fawcettsociety.org.uk/2016/01/fawcett-releases-state-of-the-nation-2016-report

Julia Gilliard

https://www.theguardian.com/commentisfree/2019/mar/08/gender-equality-not-womens-issue-good-men-too

International Women's Day

https://www.internationalwomensday.com/Theme

Rape Crisis

https://rapecrisis.org.uk/get-informed/about-sexual-violence/statistics-sexual-violence/

Janet Monckton Smith homicide research

https://www.womensaid.ie/assets/files/pdf/jane_monckton_smith_powerpoint_2018_compatibility_mode.pdf

Counting Dead Women 2018 report

https://www.theguardian.com/uk-news/2020/feb/20/over-half-of-uk-women-killed-by-men-die-hands-current-ex-partner

Domestic violence increased under lockdown

https://www.theguardian.com/society/2020/apr/27/domestic-abuse-surge-coronavirus-lockdown-lasting-impact-mps https://www.telegraph.co.uk/global-health/science-and-disease/stress-anxiety-lockdown-has-led-rise-domestic-abuse-warns/

'asymmetrical role-taking'

Det Kallas Kärlek (*It's Called Love*), Carin Holmberg (1993)

International Women's Day, Northern Ireland, March 2020

https://www.irishnews.com/news/northernirelandnews/2020/03/07/news/psni-criticised-as-female-officers-asked-to-praise-male-colleagues-on-international-women-s-day-1861402/

Andrew Moyhing case

https://www.theguardian.com/society/2006/jun/10/equality.health

Brewdog discrimination case

https://www.walesonline.co.uk/news/wales-news/i-sued-brewdog-sex-discrimination-16438100

David Madden

https://www.independent.ie/regionals/sligochampion/news/david-new-ceo-of-sligo-rape-crisis-centre-38394090.html

Caroline Flack arrest

https://metro.co.uk/2019/12/13/caroline-flack-arrested-assault-11901854/

Billy Bragg tweet

https://twitter.com/billybragg/status/1237509856547856384

Choking during sex

https://www.theatlantic.com/health/archive/2019/06/how-porn-affecting-choking-during-sex/592375/

https://www.bbc.co.uk/news/av/uk-50579537/men-have-tried-to-choke-me-during-sex

Breathplay

The Complete Manual of Breathplay, Dunter (2018) http://kinks.ca/wiki/images/8/8e/Breathplay_-_rev3.pdf

https://www.cosmopolitan.com/sex-love/a29074659/breath-play-bdsm/

Chapter 4

Audre Lorde

https://www.blackpast.org/african-american-history/speeches-
    african-american-history/1981-audre-lorde-uses-anger-women-
    responding-racism/

Intersectionality

'Demarginalizing the Intersection of Race and Sex: A Black Feminist
    Critique of Antidiscrimination Doctrine, Feminist Theory and
    Antiracist Politics', Kimberlé Crenshaw (*University of Chicago Legal
    Forum*, 1989)

Kenneth Roth tweet

https://twitter.com/KenRoth/status/630677061858930688

Sundar film

https://www.youtube.com/watch?v=wPo0MdrrF_s

'We need to talk' protest, Bristol

https://www.youtube.com/watch?v=jOB-vLia_xY

Lola Olufemi

https://medium.com/@BeaJaspert/response-to-lola-olufemis-
    statement-calling-for-supporters-of-womans-place-uk-to-be-
    excluded-from-6df7b26168cc

Paris Lees

https://www.vice.com/en_uk/article/nn97vk/ban-sex-work-fuck-off-
    white-feminism-paris-lees-807

Shon Faye and Ash Sarkar podcast

https://www.youtube.com/watch?v=86rYm6oihA4&fbclid=Iw
    AR1cQFRAxRIFzIV0zq2abViKOZdEqin60vT73TQFaLt-
    XGAlwdtEy4VQzoo

Radical suffragists

One Hand Tied Behind Us, Jill Liddington (1978)

Chapter 5

Marcie Bianco

https://qz.com/943068/the-future-of-feminism-the-gender-revolution-
has-stalled-because-feminists-think-empowement-is-more-
important-than-power/

Little Fires Everywhere (Hulu, 2020)

Christina Parreira Bunny Ranch blog

https://www.lyoncountyfreedom.org/what-theyre-saying/

'Our collective commitment'

The End of Patriarchy: Radical Feminism for Men, Robert Jensen (2016)

Zoo and Loaded

https://www.theguardian.com/media/2015/nov/22/men-behaving-
better-lads-mags-digital

Crazy, Stupid, Love (Warner Bros. Pictures, 2011)

The Onion

https://www.theonion.com/women-now-empowered-by-everything-a-
woman-does-1819566746

Emma Watson quote

https://www.buzzfeed.com/eleanorbate/emma-watson-feminism-
quotes?utm_term=.sdmPvpodZ#.rlQx65A0L

Frankie Mirren article

https://www.newstatesman.com/politics/feminism/2016/02/abortion-
sex-work-why-state-shouldn-t-control-women-s-bodies

Amnesty International Australia

https://www.amnesty.org.uk/files/my_body_my_rights_-_trainer_
campaign_briefing_0.pdf?Eld7FUasyQBgtIw7N9qrvXYCE2Ayq5ya=

Laurie Penny

https://twitter.com/pennyred/status/952648307536515073?lang=en

'gestational workers'

Full Surrogacy Now, Sophie Lewis (2019)

Chapter 6

Andrea Dworkin

In Harm's Way: The Pornography Civil Rights Hearings, Catharine Mackinnon and Andrea Dworkin (eds) (1998)

Owen Jones column

https://www.theguardian.com/commentisfree/2015/mar/30/simon-danczuk-mp-watched-porn-who-cares

Patrick Strudwick

https://twitter.com/patrickstrud/status/657924167405338625

Angela Eagle story

https://www.bbc.co.uk/news/av/uk-politics-13207256

'Feminist men'

The Achilles Heel Reader: Men, Sexual Politics and Socialism, Victor Seidler (ed) (2010)

Men's rights activists

Not Guilty: In Defence of the Modern Man, David Thomas (1993)

Richard Branson

https://www.telegraph.co.uk/news/celebritynews/5366259/Richard-Branson-defends-himself-against-claims-of-sexism.html

Trevor Mallard

https://eu.usatoday.com/story/life/parenting/2019/08/22/new-zealand-speaker-trevor-mallard-babysits-during-parliament-debate/2082213001/

Jacinda Ardern

https://www.theguardian.com/commentisfree/2018/sep/28/jacinda-ardern-baby-work-new-zealand-prime-minister-motherhood

Chapter 7

Adrienne Rich

'Compulsory Heterosexuality and Lesbian Existence', *Women: Sex and Sexuality*, Adrienne Rich (1980)

SOURCES

Guardian film

https://www.theguardian.com/commentisfree/2015/mar/12/
    dreamcatcher-prostitution-women-oppression-sex

Marcie Bianco

https://qz.com/943068/the-future-of-feminism-the-gender-revolution-
    has-stalled-because-feminists-think-empowement-is-more-
    important-than-power/

Justice for Women

https://www.justiceforwomen.org.uk/

Leeds City Council

https://www.dailymail.co.uk/news/article-6920025/The-City-change-
    gender-click-single-button.html

Diva lesbian visibility week

https://www.lesbianvisibilityweek.com/visible-lesbian-100.html#/

Jane Fae

https://www.dailymail.co.uk/femail/article-1252462/Andrea-Fletcher-
    devoted-fiancee-whos-sticking-man-John-Ozimek-despite-fact-
    wants-woman-named-Jane-Fae.html

Alex Drummond

https://www.stonewall.org.uk/trans-advisory-group

Genderbitch

https://genderbitch.wordpress.com/2009/10/30/sexuality-binarism-
    cissexism/

'Cotton ceiling'

https://medium.com/@mirandayardley/girl-dick-the-cotton-ceiling-
    and-the-cultural-war-on-lesbians-and-women-c323b4789368

Colorado lesbian 'cure'

https://www.theguardian.com/commentisfree/2018/aug/31/gay-
    conversion-therapy-the-miseducation-of-cameron-post

'political lesbianism'

*Love Your Enemy? The Debate Between Heterosexual Feminism and
    Political Lesbianism* (1981)

https://www.theguardian.com/lifeandstyle/2009/jan/30/women-gayrights

Raid on Uganda Venom bar 2016

https://www.hrw.org/news/2016/08/05/uganda-police-attack-lgbti-pride-event

https://www.truthdig.com/articles/lesbians-are-a-target-of-male-violence-the-world-over/

Is Brazil a great place to be gay?

https://www.theguardian.com/world/2019/apr/26/bolsonaro-accused-of-inciting-hatred-with-gay-paradise-comment

Brazil lesbocide

https://www.brasildefato.com.br/2018/06/05/lesbocidio-cresce-significamente-no-pais-alerta-dossie

Women attacked on a bus

https://www.theguardian.com/commentisfree/2019/jun/14/homophobic-attack-bus-outrage-media-white

https://www.independent.co.uk/news/uk/crime/london-bus-homophobic-attack-lesbian-couple-melania-geymonat-chris-hannigan-court-a9221306.html

Juno Dawson on 'passing'

https://www.theguardian.com/books/2020/may/11/juno-dawson-trans-alice-wonderland-interview-spice-girls

Chapter 8

JK Rowling

https://twitter.com/jk_rowling/status/1269389298664701952?lang=en

Clementine Ford

http://www.dailylife.com.au/news-and-views/dl-opinion/when-a-womenonly-community-is-the-answer-to-male-violence-20150817-gj109i.html

Laurie Penny tweet

https://twitter.com/PennyRed/status/653282201518346240

SOURCES

Laurie Penny Buzzfeed

https://www.buzzfeednews.com/article/lauriepenny/how-to-be-a-genderqueer-feminist

Laurie Penny on Rainbow List

https://www.independent.co.uk/news/people/therainbowlist/rainbow-list-2015-1-to-101-a6731391.html

Trans responses to Chimamanda Ngozi Adichie

https://doi-org.mmu.idm.oclc.org/10.1080/14680777.2017.1350520, Mia Fischer (2017)

Will Self

'Lesbians in men's clothing', *Evening Standard*, 29 September 2005

Scottish rape crisis

https://www.rapecrisisscotland.org.uk/links/

Karen White case

https://www.spectator.co.uk/article/why-was-a-transgender-rapist-put-in-a-women-s-prison-

https://www.theguardian.com/society/2018/oct/11/karen-white-how-manipulative-and-controlling-offender-attacked-again-transgender-prison

Fawcett Society 2016 report

https://www.fawcettsociety.org.uk/2016/01/fawcett-releases-state-of-the-nation-2016-report

Women's sports

https://www.gaystarnews.com/article/transphobic-homophobic-narratives-sports-thread/#gs.p8870x

Rachel McKinnon

https://www.thepostmillennial.com/trans-athlete-claims-lesbians-are-transphobic-for-not-liking-penises/

Martina Navratilova and Rachel McKinnon

https://www.theguardian.com/sport/2019/feb/17/martina-navratilova-criticised-over-cheating-trans-women-comments

Athlete Ally

https://www.athleteally.org/about/

Guardian report on Edinburgh attack

https://web.archive.org/web/20190606191011/https://www.
    theguardian.com/society/2019/jun/06/edinburgh-lgbt-committee-
    resigns-over-transphobic-hate-on-campus

Conclusion

Audre Lorde

'A Litany for Survival', *The Collected Poems of Audre Lorde* (1978)

Down Girl: The Logic of Misogyny, Kate Manne (2017)

Kiss Daddy Goodnight: A Speak Out on Incest, Louise Armstrong (1996)

Index

INDEX

INDEX